So Far, So Good.

A New Scoutmaster's Story

Clarke Green

First Printing January, 2015

Cover design, text, and illustrations:

© 2015 by Clarke Green

Ordering Information:
Special discounts are available on quantity purchases by corporations, associations, and others. For details, contact the publisher, Clarke Green, at www.scoutmastercg.com

This book is not an official publication of, nor is it endorsed by, the Boy Scouts of America or any other organization.

ISBN-13: 9781505790603

ISBN-10: 1505790603

Dedication

This book is for all the volunteers who care enough to make the promise of Scouting real in their communities.

Scouting is alive in every corner of the world because people of goodwill volunteer their time and resources to make it happen.

We all encounter the same challenges, setbacks, triumphs, and rewards. We are never alone.

We share the joy of serving Scouting's most important volunteers: the Scouts themselves.

Acknowledgements

None of this would be possible without the Scouts and Scouters who have so generously allowed me to be a part of their lives.

I am fortunate to have a sister, Deborah Green, who is also a supportive, dedicated, and talented editor. My deepest gratitude and love to Debbie.

I am doubly fortunate to have an understanding, supportive wife. Thank you and love to Teddi.

CONTENTS

INTRODUCTION
If I Knew then What I know Now

Scouting is not an abstruse or difficult science: rather it is a jolly game if you take it in the right light.

Robert Baden-Powell, Aids to Scoutmastership

Now that I've retired my Scoutmaster badge I'm able to write what I would have appreciated reading when I first took on the job thirty years ago.

Like any new Scouter I was, at first, concerned with the obvious, what we did at meetings, where we were going camping, how we would get there, and what we would do once we arrived.

With a young man's audacity and overconfidence I tried to imitate the slickness and regimentation I envied in some troops. I imagined myself leading an orderly column of Scouts on parade, and having folks tell each other what a great guy I was.

I was anxious to look the part. I bought a campaign hat and a red jacket, and admired the patches and decorations other Scouters wore.

None of those things made me a better Scouter, and some of the attitudes I adopted made me insufferably self-important.

Eventually I became much more interested in doing actual good rather than just looking the part. I wanted to be useful rather than simply chasing the appearance of success. I began to ask myself how, exactly, this game played in the outdoors benefitted young people. What could I do to make the most of my opportunity as a Scouter?

Some of the answers came from older, more experienced Scouters, some from the Scouts themselves, some from working through my many mistakes and missteps; but the real revelation was stumbling on the writings of Scouting's founder, Robert Baden-Powell.

B-P had a knack for getting at the heart of things. His brief, but meaningful "Aids to Scoutmastership" is required reading for any Scouter.

Ten years ago, I started writing a blog at ScoutmasterCG.com. I gained a small readership, and started fielding questions. I struggled to write clearly and offer useful advice. I finally hit on the idea of telling a story to illustrate what I have come to understand about over the past three decades.

What would I do if I had the chance to start all over again? What if I knew then what I know now?

Most of our training courses and official literature present an idealized, sanitized, and artificial picture of Scouting. We'd all like to think Scouting is like the images we see in Norman Rockwell paintings; but being a Scoutmaster means working with real people.

Real people argue, Scouts misbehave, parents overreact, Scouters get discouraged, and little goes as smoothly as those idealized images would have you believe.

After some years, I stopped trying to imitate an idealized picture and started helping Scouts discover authentic Scouting for themselves. We all stand on the shoulders of just over a century of Scouting's combined experience. There are no new problems; we all encounter the same challenges, and all of us muddle through as best we can.

If you are expecting a book full of systematic instructions or closely defined policy statements, you are going to be disappointed. You'll find that getting the policies and procedures right isn't all that difficult. Scouting is not quite like anything else young people do; catching the spirit of our work is a bigger challenge. Once you have a handle on why we do what we do as Scouters, the policies and procedures begin to make sense; they become nearly intuitive.

I lay no claim that what you'll read is the only authentic way of doing things, or even that I am close to having everything right. Troops are like families, they have different ways of functioning, their own quirks and traditions. So long as Scouters do no harm, I think any child can get a lot out of being a Scout.

This narrative loosely follows my own experiences, but the new Scoutmaster in the story begins knowing things that took me many years to understand. All the names are altered, but there are enough clues here and there that some of my old Scouts and fellow Scouters may recognize themselves.

What I have written does not bear the endorsement of any Scouting organization. I wrote it with the hope you'll find it useful, and inspire you to discover something more about the spirit of your work as a Scouter.

CHAPTER ONE
No Turning Back!

Do not be appalled by any imaginary magnitude of the task. It will disappear when once you see the aim.

B-P, *Aids to Scoutmastership*

If I had a nickel for every time I thought, said or heard the phrase "so far so good" over the past few months I'd be a rich man. I'd served as an assistant Scoutmaster for a few years when our Scoutmaster announced a job relocation that required his family to move.

Mark Hacker, our committee chair, took me aside one evening and asked me if I would consider being the new Scoutmaster.

I was stunned.

I love Scouting, it's great fun. But, really?

I told Mark I would have to think about it.

I watched our old Scoutmaster do it all for the past few years, and I admired his dedication; but could *I* actually take this on?

My son was a Scout, and he got a lot out of our troop. He graduated high school this spring, and enters college in the fall.

My wife Anne and I discussed the commitments involved, the time away camping and attending meetings. Anne appreciated what Scouts did for our son and believes in the program. She agreed I ought to give it a try (no doubt, she'd also miss the one weekend a month she's grown used to having to herself over the past few years!)

After we talked it through, I called Mark and told him I would take the job in the fall. I had three months to prepare, so I started reading everything I could find about Scouting. Before long I concluded our old Scoutmaster probably did too much.

He and the other adults planned all the meetings and outings, appointed the senior patrol leader, decided which Scouts should be in what patrol, and chose their patrol leaders. Our assistant Scoutmasters did all the instructing, and shadowed the youth leadership to the extent the Scouts were leaders in name only.

Several years ago I took a training course that laid things out much differently than the way our troop did things. I was curious about why our troop didn't follow what they told me in training, so I asked.

"I'll tell you what the last Scoutmaster told me:" our Scoutmaster answered emphatically, "He said 'what they tell you in training and what *actually works* are two different things.' He showed me how he ran things, and what he did worked for twelve years, so that's what we do."

At the time it made sense. Who was I to say different? I was just the "new guy." It was our practice to have assistant Scoutmasters take turns planning and running meetings and a camping trip every month.

The first time I was in charge I understood what the Scoutmaster said! I couldn't imagine our boys planning or presiding over an orderly troop meeting, much less planning and carrying out a camping trip.

The more I studied the Scoutmaster's job, though, the more sure I became that we'd better serve our Scouts if we made some changes. When I sat down with Mark, our committee chair, to lay out these ideas he was skeptical; what I suggested would be considerably different.

After several discussions, we agreed that we would back each other up and make the changes I suggested. Mark asked our committee to agree to this arrangement, they did, and we were off and running.

A couple of weeks before I was to take over I sat down with our four assistant Scoutmasters. I mapped out the changes I discussed with Mark.

Dave Stanley, who had been around longer than any of us, was the first to reply, saying: "I think we owe Chuck at least the benefit of the doubt; after all, none of us took the job, did we?"

"I appreciate that, Dave," I replied, "all I am asking is that you guys follow my lead. The changes we've discussed are significant and I expect some skepticism; but I need your support."

"It all kind of makes sense to me," said George Hudson, "I am willing to work with you."

"Me too," Wayne Murray chimed in, "I think the Scouts can do at least some of what you've said."

"I didn't want the job," said Rob Borgatti, "As long as nobody interferes I'll be happy to keep doing what I do with the gear."

I left the meeting with a strange combination of excitement and dread. It was like stepping off the edge and jumping into a volcano; no turning back now!

CHAPTER TWO
First Troop Meeting

The Scoutmaster guides the boy in the spirit of an older brother.

B-P, *Aids to Scoutmastership*

"Before we go any further," I said, "I am interested in how you would answer some questions, because what you have to say is important." I invited five Scouts to speak with me at my first meeting as their new Scoutmaster. They were our oldest Scouts and, although adults had been doing nearly everything for them, I saw some leadership potential in each.

"So my first question is: how should we decide who is going to be our next senior patrol leader?"

The Scouts looked at each other, the floor, the ceiling, and the table.

Utter silence.

Jake Hendricks finally said, "You pick them, right?"

"That's how we've done it in the past," I answered, "are you guys happy with doing things that way?"

They stared at me as if I had lost my mind.

Well, I thought, at least I had their attention.

"How else would it work?" Zach asked.

"You tell me Zach," I handed him my opened Scoutmaster Handbook (I had put many bookmarks in my copy over the past couple of months), "read the first couple of sentences on that page."

"The youth leader with the most responsibility in a troop is the senior patrol leader. He is elected by all members of the troop," Zach read, he looked up, "huh, interesting."

Several conversations started spontaneously as the Scouts discussed the pluses and minuses of electing a senior patrol leader.

"Mr. Grant, are we allowed to do it like that?" Jake asked.

"Before I answer that question, how many of you have played basketball?" I asked.

The Scouts exchanged more confused looks, but they all raised their hands.

"Bob," I said, "why is a basketball hoop ten feet high?"

Bob jumped a little, "I guess there's a rule?" he replied.

"I think you're right," I said, "is a Scout troop kind of like a basketball team?" I asked no one in particular.

"We have uniforms," Zach offered, "and we play games, but not always basketball."

"Anything else?" I asked.

"I guess we have rules?" said Jake.

"Where are the rules, then?" I asked Jake, helpfully tapping on my Scoutmaster handbook.

"Oh, I get it now," Jake turned to the other Scouts, "this is kind of like a rule book," he said pointing to the Scoutmaster's handbook.

"So let me ask my first question again," I said, "how do we decide who is going to be our next senior patrol leader?"

"He is elected by all the members of the troop," Zach replied, "because that's in the rules."

We discussed how the election should happen, who would run, and within five or ten minutes, the Scouts had come up with a plan.

"So Jake and Bob are your candidates," I started reviewing their decisions, "are we sure nobody else is interested?"

The Scouts shook their heads.

I continued, "Zach, Alex, and Hunter are going to hand out the ballots and pencils, and hand them to me when you are all done, right?"

The Scouts nodded yes.

"I'll say a couple of things first," I went on, "then Jake and Zach will each have a minute or two to say why they want to be senior patrol leader, then you'll have your election."

With that, we walked out into the meeting room where the rest of the Scouts were watching Dave Stanley show them how to sharpen a pocketknife.

"Ready Mr. G?" he asked when he saw us enter the room.

"Thanks Mr. S," I replied, and stepped to the front of the room. I told the Scouts they would be electing a fellow Scout to lead them for the next few months as their senior patrol leader. I described how important the decision was, and introduced their candidates. After each spoke, I stepped to the back of the room as the Scouts received their ballots and prepared to vote.

George and Wayne, two more assistant Scoutmasters, were lying in wait.

"How did it go?" George asked.

"They got the idea pretty quickly," I answered, "they're a sharp bunch."

"Hunter didn't want to run?" Wayne asked with an edge of disappointment.

"I asked them all," I said, "he never spoke up, and I asked everyone a second time just to be sure, but he said no."

"Well, there's always next time around I guess," Wayne sighed.

"Listen, dad, he'll be fine," I said patting Wayne on the back, "give him a little time."

"Here are the ballots Mr. G," said Alex, holding out a rumpled pile of paper.

"Thanks Alex," I said taking them, "Dave, you and I don't have dogs in this fight, would you give me a hand for a moment?" (Dave's boy was two years ahead of my son in college.)

I turned to George and Wayne, "keep them busy for a moment, this won't take long."

Dave and I stepped into the next room, counted the votes, and returned.

When it was time to close the meeting I stepped to the front of the room, and a few seconds later we had a new senior patrol leader.

One change made, only a couple hundred more to go!

CHAPTER THREE
Second Troop Meeting

Scouting is a game for boys, under the leadership of boys

B-P, Aids to Scoutmastership

The Scouts elected Jake Hendricks as their senior patrol leader; I think they made a great choice. At 14, Jake isn't the oldest Scout, but he showed a lot of potential.

I asked Jake and the four older Scouts I spoke with last week to meet with me thirty minutes before the next troop meeting.

"I had another question for you," I began, "where are we going camping next month?"

"You were going to tell us tonight, right?" Jake replied.

"Did anyone ever ask you where you wanted to go or what you wanted to do?" I asked.

They thought about that one for a moment.

"We talk about stuff," Jake said, "but usually the Scoutmasters tell us."

"Jake," I asked, "If you could take the troop anywhere, or do anything you wanted to do, what would that be?"

He didn't have to think about it, "Mountain climbing! Mr. Callas [our previous Scoutmaster] always said it was too dangerous."

"Okay," I said, "let's go mountain climbing!"

"Really, that would be awesome!" Hunter said, "Are we really allowed to do that?"

"Where do you think we could find the answer to your question Hunter?" I asked.

"The rule book?" Hunter answered.

"Let's look in the Scout Handbook this time," I said, "anybody have one?"

Bob held up his copy.

"Great, thanks Bob," I said, "read the introduction in the very beginning for us."

Bob read the first few paragraphs aloud.

"Sounds like Scouts go camping and do adventurous things," I said, "I think mountain climbing fits that description."

"Can we get a badge for it?" Zach asked.

"There is a climbing merit badge; I'd imagine you could at least get started on that," I replied, "what you'll find is that when we do what Scouts do requirements are kind of built in. When we plan what we'll be doing we want to choose what Scouts do, because then you'll have the opportunity to advance."

"Makes sense," Bob said.

"So the choice for this month is mountain climbing," I said, "anybody object?"

They all shook their heads.

"That's settled," I said, "I have a couple of other questions."

The Scouts looked at me expectantly.

"We usually set up new patrols this time of year," I began, "how would you guys like to do that?"

"What's the rule book say?" Zach asked.

"I thought you'd never ask!" I said hauling the Scoutmaster handbook out of my backpack, finding my bookmark, opening it, and handing it to Zach.

"Wow," Zach said, "that's a whole page, do I have to read all that?"

"I have a couple of other things to do for the next few minutes," I said walking away, "Look things over and see if you Scouts can figure out what to do next."

I wanted to see, while I did a lap around the building, how much they could figure out on their own.

"So?" I asked when I returned, "What's the plan Jake?"

"We know a little bit more about what the 'rule book' says about patrols," he answered, "but there are no directions."

"Sort of like basketball," I remarked, "the rules tell you about the game, but you have to actually play the game yourself to understand it."

The stares I received in response were a little less confused.

"Let's attack this question a step at a time," I began, "Who will decide who goes in what patrol?"

"I guess I could," said Jake.

"Okay, sounds good," I replied, "What do you need to know to make good decisions? Bob what do you think?"

"How old everyone is?" he offered.

"That would help. Anything else?" I replied.

"Maybe ranks?" Zach added.

"Good, anything else?" I prodded.

Hunter cleared his throat, and quietly added, "I don't know about you guys but I know what patrol I'd like to be in, I'd like to be with my friends and stuff."

"I think all the Scouts feel that way, Hunter," I said, "how would you guys go about making that happen?"

Over the next few minutes, we discussed sorting out patrols. I suggested that they have each Scout write down the name of three other Scouts they'd like to have in their patrol. Jake would take those lists and work out the best lineup for each patrol.

"Last question, guys, I promise," I said, "how are you going to figure out who the patrol leaders will be?"

"Rule book please!" Zach said and held out his hand.

I smiled, "Right here at this marker," I said handing him the Scoutmaster's handbook.

We were done a few minutes before troop meeting time. I left the picnic table and joined my assistant Scoutmasters in the back of the room.

"You and your secret meetings," said George, "what's all this skullduggery leading to?"

"Yeah," added Wayne, "I am feeling like you are keeping us in the dark."

"It's all his master plan for world domination," George said rubbing his hands together.

"C'mon guys, I told you last week," I said, "blabber-mouths like you two can't be trusted with sensitive information."

Dave laughed at the three of us, "Alright, Mister Scoutmaster, spill the beans."

"Okay, you got me," I said, "am I trying your patience a little?"

"A little?" said George.

"First, I appreciate you were willing to let me meet with these guys on my own." I started, "they are starting to think things through on their own, besides…"

"We can't keep our mouths shut!" said George.

"Well, to put it bluntly, yes." I said, "You know what would happen if all four of us were sitting at the table, right?"

"Yeah," Wayne sighed, and turned to George "the new guy is right, but I still hate him."

"Well, you'll get over it." I laughed, "at least I hope so."

"So it went well?" Wayne asked seriously.

"Let's listen in and see," I replied.

Jake was doing his best to get everyone's attention, and eventually the Scouts quieted down enough to hear him.

The older Scouts handed out index cards and pencils and Jake asked each Scout to list three others they'd like to have in their patrol.

A few minutes later Jake collected the cards. I asked Dave to come help Jake and me while Wayne and George led the Scouts in a game.

"Bob wants to be in the same patrol as Ian," Jake said looking at one list.

"Does Ian's list have Bob on it?" I asked.

Jake looked through the cards, "Yes, he has Bob, Brian and Drew."

"So that's a good match," Dave replied, "who do Brain and Drew want?"

We laid the cards out on the picnic table, matching Scouts into three patrols so each had at least one of their choices.

"Anybody left?" I asked.

"Nobody had Jason on their list." Jake replied.

"Can you put him with a least one of his choices?" Dave asked.

"If I do," Jake replied, "the numbers will be uneven."

"Is it important to have even numbers?" I asked.

"I thought they had to be even," said Jake.

"I guess it's all nice and neat of they are, but what's more important to you," I asked, "even patrols or the Scout's choices?"

Jake did a little rearranging and incorporated Jason into a patrol with one of the Scouts he listed.

"Before you go tell everyone who is in what Patrol." I said looking at Jake, "I want to point out that you'll end up knowing a few things as senior patrol leader that you'll want to keep confidential."

"Like what?" Jake asked.

"Well, nobody chose Jason for their patrol," I replied, "How do you think he'd feel if he knew that?"

"I suppose not so great," Jake replied.

"Yeah," Dave said, "let's keep that between the three of us."

"Knowing this," I said to Jake, "means that you can look out for Jason, and see what you can do to help him find some friends too."

As Jake went in to announce the new patrol lineup, I huddled with my Assistant Scoutmasters.

"More secrets?" George said.

"Not for long," I replied.

"It made sense for you and Dave to do that since your sons have moved on," Wayne said, "I hope Hunter is happy with the new setup. Who did you pick for patrol leaders?"

"Each patrol will elect one before we leave tonight." I said.

"You and your 'democracy'," George said, "you'd think we were teaching Scouts about citizenship or something!"

"Well," I laughed, "glad you are catching on!"

CHAPTER FOUR
First Committee Meeting

Occasionally, difficulties may loom up so as almost to blot out the radiant possibilities. But it is comforting to remember that they are generally out of their proper proportion and subside as you approach them.

B-P, *Aids to Scoutmastership*

"Mountain climbing!" Barry, our membership chair was surprised, "Is that safe?"

"Sounds expensive," added Fran, our treasurer.

"Our Scouts call it 'mountain climbing,' what we'll be doing is called 'bouldering,'" I replied, "There's a great spot at Kitterich State Park and I've asked one of the counselors who instructs climbing merit badge to help us out."

"So the boys will earn climbing merit badge?" Fran asked.

"They will all get a good idea of what it takes," I replied, "and the Scouts who are interested in earning the badge can make arrangements with the counselor."

"Shouldn't we choose a badge for this month that they can complete?' asked Fran.

"I think it's important that this idea came from the Scouts," I gave Mark, our committee chair, a knowing glance, "Besides, I don't plan on having merit badge instruction or work at our meetings quite like we have in the past."

"Well, what will the Scouts do instead?" Fran asked.

"Sounds like mountain climbing or boulders, or whatever, is a waste of time," said Barry, "If they don't earn a badge what's the point?"

"The point is getting them doing what Scouts do," I replied, "because when they do those things advancement and learning come naturally."

I got the same response I had from my older Scouts, a slightly confused stare.

"Don't Scouts 'do' merit badges?" asked Linda, the advancement chair, "I don't understand what you are saying."

"Yes, merit badges are part of what Scouts do," I replied, "but there are other aspects of Scouting we can develop."

"Maybe you could explain that a little," said Mark, "what other aspects?"

"For one I have been working closely with our patrol leaders' council," I replied, "to provide them with the opportunity to make decisions and take on more responsibility for their troop."

I told the committee how we elected our new senior patrol leader, set up patrols, and elected patrol leaders. I fielded many questions about those changes over the next fifteen minutes.

"I know this is all a little different from what we are used to," I smiled, "let me get through this month and next month we'll see how things went."

Barry turned to Mark, "Isn't the committee's job making these sorts of decisions?" he asked, "these are serious changes, and I think we ought to vote on them before we go any further."

Mark leaned back in his chair, "Chuck and I discussed this, I discussed his ideas with the committee, and the committee followed my recommendation that he become our Scoutmaster."

"Yes, but, I don't think we had any idea that things would change so drastically," Barry said.

"Some of us, and I say 'us' because that includes me," Mark replied, "have grown used to one way of doing things. I'd hazard a guess it's been quite some time since any of us have actually read some of the resources we received when we were trained several years ago."

"C'mon, Mark," Barry asked impatiently, "what are you getting at?"

"What I am saying is the changes Chuck is making are perfectly consistent with the Scouting program," he said, "He's done his homework. I've checked it out, and I'm telling you that we have drifted a bit over the years, Chuck is working to put us back on track."

"But we haven't voted on any of this!" Barry said.

"As soon as you can show me, in black and white," Mark replied, "where a committee is empowered to pick what parts of the Scouting program we decide to follow and what parts we don't I'll be happy to have a vote."

The discussion went on for a while. At times, it was a little heated, heated enough that I was almost ready to get up and leave my Scoutmaster patch on the table.

With Mark's guidance, most of the committee came around, but a few remained seriously skeptical.

When the meeting concluded, Mark caught up with me in the parking lot.

"I think that went well," he said, "I admire your self-control."

"Thanks Mark," I replied, "I appreciate your support."

"I meant what I said," he replied, "we'll back each other up and just keep on keeping on."

"So far so good?" I asked.

"So far so good!" he replied.

I called Jake to let him know our 'mountain' climbing trip was approved, "Spread the word, call your patrol leaders, and let's see how many Scouts we can get to Monday's meeting."

"I'll do my best," Jake replied.

CHAPTER FIVE
With the Patrol Leaders

The Patrol System is the one essential feature in which Scout training differs from that of all other organizations, and where the System is properly applied, it is absolutely bound to bring success. It cannot help itself!

B-P, *Aids to Scoutmastership*

When Monday rolled around Jake and two patrol leaders were waiting when I pulled into the parking lot.

"Hey guys, ready for a little mountain climbing?"

Jake smiled, "You bet!"

"I've set it up for the camping trip we have planned next month," I said, " that means after tonight we have three troop meetings to get ready and you guys have a lot to do."

The Scouts seemed puzzled; a look I had come to expect.

Our third patrol leader showed up and we headed for the picnic table.

"I think it'll be a good idea for you guys to get together like this every week," I began, "this is our 'patrol leaders' council.'"

"Let me guess," Zach said, "that's in the rule book, right?"

"Jake," I asked, "have you got it?"

"I almost forgot," Jake pulled the copy of the Senior Patrol Leader's Handbook I gave him last week from his book bag.

"It's right here," Jake said as he handed the opened book to Zach.

"I have a few questions for the patrol leaders' council." I began, "In three weeks we are going camping on our mountain climbing trip. What do you figure we should take along?"

Jake looked puzzled, "Uh, I guess what we usually take along."

"So what is that exactly?" I asked.

"Tents and stuff?" Hunter answered.

"Right," I replied, "I suppose you guys would like to eat while you are there too?"

"Yeah," Hunter replied cautiously.

"So who is going to make sure we have everything we need when we get there?" I asked.

Jake thought for a moment, "Well the adults bring the food I guess, and the tents and stuff."

"That's how we have done things in the past," I said, "Could we do things differently this time?"

The Scouts exchanged looks, "I guess so," Jake replied.

"How about if each patrol gets their own food and cooks it by themselves?" I asked.

"Sounds like a lot of work," Hunter replied, "we haven't all done cooking merit badge yet."

"If you kept it simple it wouldn't be too much of a problem, right?" I asked.

"I suppose, maybe," Zach replied uncertainly, "we could try it out."

"Maybe we could talk about cooking at a meeting?" Jake asked.

"I think that's a great idea," I answered, "the patrol leaders' council is in charge of what goes on at meetings. If you like, I'll ask Mr. Hudson to help out with that tonight, okay?"

The Scouts nodded a little skeptically.

"Here's what I think happens next," I continued, "when we open our meeting tonight Jake can announce that we are going mountain climbing and that each patrol will be cooking their own food. You patrol leaders get your patrols together and figure out a menu for the weekend, and we'll go from there."

Jake still looked a little puzzled, "Okay, you want me to say all that?"

"Well, you are the senior patrol leader," I encouraged, "so I think you ought to get to do a little leading, what do you think?"

I walked Jake through making a few notes, and he did a good job of getting things going when the troop meeting opened a few minutes later.

More change, more momentum, I only hoped I could keep up.

CHAPTER SIX
Third Troop Meeting

If you make listening and observation your particular occupation, you will gain much more information from your boys than you can put into them by your own talk.

B-P, *Aids to Scoutmastership*

I corralled my assistant Scoutmasters, Wayne, George, and Dave, in one corner of the meeting room.

"As you heard our senior patrol leader announce a moment ago," I began, "the patrols are working on some plans for the weekend."

"Uh oh," Wayne turned to George, "more new stuff!"

"After all he is the new guy," George said.

"Yes, I am," I smiled.

"Think they will actually be able to eat what they cook?" asked George.

"Nobody cooks a well as you do, George," I replied patting George on the shoulder, "but they'll figure things out, and that's the point, right?"

George shook his head, "No, I'm serious; I don't think we can expect much, most of these boys haven't even been through cooking merit badge yet."

"How did you learn to cook George?" I asked,

"I watched my dad, and he showed me a few things." George replied.

"But at some point you had to actually put something in a pan …" I said.

George laughed and broke in, "… and burn it to a crisp."

"Yes, but the second time you knew better, right?" I asked.

"Well maybe after the third or fourth try," George relied.

"But you get my point; I want the Scouts doing things we are used to doing for them." I looked around at all three of them, "I know that you guys are at least a little skeptical about this."

"A little?" Wayne said.

"Let's see how things go," I said, "all I am asking is that you play along and follow my lead, okay?"

"I can't remember a boy starving to death over a weekend." Dave said.

"Was this your idea;" Wayne asked, "or did the Scouts come up with it?"

"I suggested the idea," I replied, "and I pushed them a little."

"But aren't they supposed to be coming up with things by themselves?" Wayne asked "Isn't that what 'boy-led' is all about?"

"Eventually, yes," I replied, "the Scouts will begin to take the initiative on these things, but I am doing what I can to get them headed in the right direction."

"I guess the trick is knowing when to make suggestions, when to give directions, and when to wait for them to sort things out." Dave added.

"I think that says it, Dave," I replied, "I doubt I'll get everything right to begin with."

"But so far so good," Dave said, "At least as far as I can tell."

"You read my mind," I replied, "so far so good!"

I asked George to spend ten or fifteen minutes going over some cooking basics in the Scout Handbook later that evening.

It seemed like the Scouts were all talking at once, there was little visible order. Jake looked a little overwhelmed.

I walked over to Jake, "Looks like things are going pretty well, what do you think?"

"Everybody's pretty excited about making up menus and stuff, they're just a little loud," he replied.

"Tell your patrol leaders that they have five more minutes," I said, "and then get everybody back together, Mr. Hudson will take it from there while we have a quick huddle with the patrol leaders' council."

I turned away from Jake just in time to see our committee chair come through the door.

"Hey Mark, how are you?" I asked as I shook his hand.

"I'm fine, thanks," Mark surveyed the scene, he looked a little pale, "what's going on?"

"The patrols are working on menus for their mountain climbing trip." I replied.

"Awfully loud in here," Mark mumbled as he fumbled through his briefcase.

"I have permission slips for your trip," he said, "I only have time to hand them out, and then I have to get going."

Mark started for the middle of the room. I knew what came next; he'd call for attention and talk about the permission slips for about ten minutes.

I stopped him, "Thanks Mark, let me take those and I'll be sure the Scouts get them before they leave."

"I can do this, it's okay," he replied, a little confused.

"Actually, Mark, I'd rather that you didn't this time." I said, "I promise I'll take care of things, and the Scouts will have the slips back to you next week as usual."

Mark smiled wryly, and looked down his nose at me, "Okay, new guy, I'll try it your way this time. Just be sure to remind them…"

"…to have their parent's give us an emergency phone number." I filled in. I had heard Mark say this dozens of times.

"Exactly," Mark said, "they always forget to do that," he looked at his watch, "I do have to run, best of luck Mr. Scoutmaster."

"Thanks again, Mark," I replied.

While I was heading the committee chair off at the pass, Jake had assembled the troop, and was looking at me expectantly.

"What happens next?" I asked him.

"Oh yeah," turning to the Scouts he said, "Mr. Hudson is going to do cooking now."

"And …" I started.

"Oh, yeah," Jake said, "I need patrol leaders over here."

I led the patrol leaders' council outside to the picnic table.

"So how did menu planning go?" I asked.

Silence.

I turned to one of the patrol leaders: "Bob, what is your patrol having for breakfast on Saturday?"

Bob jumped a little, "uh, pancakes I think."

"Sounds great, Bob, what do you need to make pancakes?"

Bob jumped again, "Pancake stuff?"

"So I get a box of pancake stuff, then what?" I asked

Bob jumped a third time, "Then you make pancakes."

"What do I put in the pan before I make pancakes?"

Bob had no idea what I was driving at, "What?" he asked.

"Don't you put butter or something in the pan first?" Jake asked.

"Now you are catching on!" I said, "Bob, I hope you don't feel like I am picking on you, I am just trying to help you guys think this through. Did anybody write their menu down?"

Zach had some notes, but the other two were relying on their memory. We discussed things for a few more minutes. When we got up from the table, the patrol leaders had figured out that a menu in writing would help things along, and they'd need some idea of what they needed to cook the menu.

"One last thing," I said, "how many of you can meet me at the grocery store one evening this week so we can go shopping?"

We spent a moment discussing arrangements for grocery shopping.

As they headed in the door, I handed Jake the permission slips, "These need to go home with every Scout tonight, can you be sure that happens?"

"No problem," Jake said, "I'll tell them."

"Remember you have patrol leaders," I said.

Jake looked at me quizzically, for a second, then he smiled, "you mean give these to the patrol leaders?"

"And they can give them to their Scouts." I said, "It's a small thing, but it's important, from here on out everything happens by patrol."

"Got it!" Jake replied.

"After you get done at the closing I have some things to say if that's okay." I asked.

"Sure," Jake replied and started through the door.

"Oh, yeah," I said, "I almost forgot; be sure to tell everybody to make sure their parents put..."

"...the emergency phone number on the permission slips," Jake finished for me, "yeah, I know."

CHAPTER SEVEN
At the Grocery Store

So, too, in giving instruction it is better by far to get your boys to debate a point or to ask you questions than to preach information to them. There's a lot to be got by listening and observing.

B-P's Outlook

I called Jake and the three patrol leaders about our meeting at the grocery store. "Make sure to bring your menus, otherwise we won't know what to get," I reminded them.

I asked George Hudson and Wayne Murray two of my assistant Scoutmasters, to come along. George was able to make it, but Wayne couldn't. I asked George to stick with me while the Scouts shopped.

Once we were all together, we huddled outside the grocery store for a moment. "Okay, let's take a look at your menus," I turned to Bob, "still pancakes for breakfast on Saturday?"

Bob didn't startle quite as much, "Yeah, still pancakes."

"So what do you need to…?"

"… Pancake mix and butter!" Bob said.

"Good for you, now you're talking! So no syrup on those pancakes?" I asked.

Bob grimaced, got a pen out of his pocket and scribbled on his menu as the other Scouts laughed.

"Now you are getting the idea!" I said, "Let me show you something," I showed them the menu I had prepared to feed the adults on camping trip, "See? Here's the menu, and here's everything I need to cook it; that's my shopping list."

I went briefly explained the concept of the shopping list, and the Scouts seemed to catch on.

"Jake, your job tonight is making sure everyone else does theirs, okay?" I asked.

Jake nodded.

"Mr. Hudson and I will be there if you have questions," I continued, "each of you get a cart, and we'll all meet at the checkout in a half hour or so."

The Scouts took off.

George looked at me, "That's it?"

"What's it?" I asked.

"Those boys have no idea what they are doing, I can't wait to see what they get," he chuckled, "when I do cooking merit badge we go into a lot more detail than that."

"George," I said, "Hold on to your hat, I am going to boss you around for a moment."

"SIR, yes SIR!" George returned an exaggerated salute.

"I want you to listen as I work with the Scouts at first," I directed, "and try not to talk; if that's even humanly possible."

George put both hands over his mouth.

"You should learn how to do that more often," I laughed, "that's a good look for you."

George punched me in the arm.

We caught up with one of the patrol leaders, "Hey Bob, how many Scouts in your patrol are going on the trip?" I asked.

"Five, I think," he replied.

I looked in Bob's shopping cart, "I see you have a one pound box of spaghetti for dinner, does that look alike enough to you?"

"I don't know, maybe?" he said.

"Take a look at the box;" I said, "do you see anything about servings anywhere?"

"Serving size four ounces," he read.

"Four times five is 20 right?" Bob nodded, "how many ounces in a pound?"

"Sixteen," Bob replied.

"So…?" I asked.

George started to answer, I shot him a look, and he put his hands over his mouth.

"I need more spaghetti," Bob said.

"There you go! You'll have enough for more than five according to the box, but I'll be you guys will be pretty hungry after all that climbing," I said.

Bob headed off and I called out, "you going to have sauce on that?"

"Yes," he answered over his shoulder, "I'll get enough too!"

I turned to George, "That's exactly what I'd like you to do, ask questions instead of giving directions or answers."

"I'll give it a try, I still think we are going to have some hungry Scouts," George replied, "we could have told them all this before we started, you know."

"You're right," I said, "but my plan is to work along with them, step by step, at first, like I'm doing now," I explained," to get them in the habit of figuring things out for themselves."

"Huh," George said, "seems like a lot more work to me."

"At first it will be," I replied, "but we are building something we haven't had before."

George's son Zach came down the aisle, "Dad, how much oatmeal should I get?"

"Hey Zach," I said stepping between him and his father, "I was just talking to Bob about that a moment ago, ask him about serving sizes."

Zach looked at me, then at his father, back at me again, "Okay...I guess,"

"Go find Bob," George said.

I patted George on the back, "see, it's not that hard is it?"

George smiled, "it's a little different, that's for sure, but you are the Scoutmaster," he saluted again, "and I'll do as I am told, for now."

George and I circulated and asked plenty of questions for the next half hour.

After we checked out, they marked their patrol name on each bag as we put them in my van.

"I'll put these in our store room, and put refrigerated stuff in the refrigerator at our meeting place." I said, "Each patrol will need a cooler for the weekend, okay?"

The Scouts nodded, "It takes some practice, but you guys did a great job figuring things out and sticking to your budget," I said.

As we waited for the rest to be picked up, George and I talked.

"I think that went pretty well," said George, "maybe I can even get Zach to do all the family grocery shopping."

"I don't know about that," I laughed, "but I do think the Scouts are ready to take on things like this and more."

"This whole asking questions thing is tiring for me," George said, "but I have to admit it works."

"If we help them figure things out for themselves," I said, "eventually they develop the habit of finding answers without us."

George chuckled, "Zach wants to know if he'll get a badge for all this."

"He already has a patrol leader's patch right?" I replied.

"Touché!" said George, "but seriously, aren't they completing requirements for ranks or merit badges by doing this?"

"Yes, they are," I answered, "but what I'd like us to start thinking about is the difference between working on requirements and doing what Scouts do."

"Aren't they basically the same?" George asked.

"Yes, all the rank requirements refer to things Scouts do." I said, "What I am saying is that instead of starting out trying to complete a requirement we just do what Scouts do, and advancement is a side-effect."

"I think I see what you're saying," George said, "makes sense I suppose."

"Look at all the fun they had this evening, and we didn't mention requirements once," I said.

"Yeah, they just kind of naturally got interested in the whole thing," George observed,

"And we just trained all of our patrol leaders to go grocery shopping," I added, "next time they can show one of the Scouts in their patrol how to do it without us."

"You may just make a Scoutmaster yet," George said.

"Maybe," I replied, "but only if you keep quiet."

George punched me in the arm again.

CHAPTER EIGHT
Fourth Troop Meeting

It is almost beyond belief that grown-up, or nearly grown-up, men can take little matters so seriously and so narrowly as some of them do.

B-P's Outlook

Two weeks before our mountain climbing trip I sat at the picnic table with our patrol leaders' council. Jake and I had exchanged several emails and talked on the phone a few times since we last met. We discussed appointing a quartermaster, and Jake chose Alex Monroe, the last of the five older Scouts I originally met with who had yet to take on a specific responsibility.

Jake had been preparing for what came next and he looked like he was ready to get things moving.

"I have a couple of things to do, so Jake is going to let you know what happens at tonight's meeting." I said,

"Alex, I'll get together with you and Mr. Borgatti when the patrols are meeting."

Alex nodded, and with that, I walked away from the table.

"Tonight we need to figure out two things: what your patrol needs for the camping trip, and what each Scout should bring," Jake began, "the lists of what to bring for Scouts is in the Handbook, right here," Jake held up an opened handbook.

"I want you guys to write down what your patrol will need on these cards." Jake handed each patrol leader an index card, "and pick out one Scout to be your patrol quartermaster."

As Jake worked with the patrol leaders' council, I met Rob Borgatti, my fourth assistant Scoutmaster, as he pulled into the parking lot. Only Dave Stanley had been around longer than Rob, who had settled into being our "gear guru."

Rob looked after the troop gear, made sure it showed up when we were camping, and that it all made its way home again. He had made it very clear to me he wasn't interested in doing more than that.

"Let me get this straight, the Scouts are going to tell me what to bring?" Rob was not happy.

"Yes, we'll have a quartermaster to see that they get what they need," I said.

"We don't need a quartermaster and I don't want one," Rob said, "we tried that years ago and it didn't work."

"Our senior patrol leader has appointed Alex Monroe to be the quartermaster," I replied, "Jake and I have been working on that since last week."

Rob grunted and walked over to the equipment room.

I headed back to the picnic table, "Everything good?" I asked Jake.

"I think so," he replied.

"Hunter, what page is the Scout gear list on in the handbook?" I asked.

Hunter looked at his notes, "page 274."

"Great, sounds like you guys are ready to meet with your patrols," I said, "remember we need your patrol list along with your patrol quartermaster when you finish patrol meetings tonight."

Only two meetings in, Jake was finding his feet as senior patrol leader. He managed to get the troop assembled and listening while I corralled my assistant Scoutmasters in the back of the room.

"Everybody has something to do right?" I asked,

"Yes Sir!" George shouted, as he delivered his exaggerated salute.

"So Wayne will be keeping George quiet," I laughed, "it's a big job, buddy but I think you are up to it."

Wayne glared at George, and George made himself as small as possible.

"Seriously though," I went on, "as soon as Jake has opened the meeting what happens next?"

"I've got all the stuff on the list in the handbook to show them," George said.

"I'll show them how to pack a pack," Wayne said.

"And I'll talk about tents." Dave added.

"Right, three patrols rotating through three stations, ten minutes at each station, Jake will be keeping time and telling everyone when to change stations." I said.

As the stations were going on, I talked to Jake.

"So far so good?" I asked.

"Yeah, pretty good, but some of the older guys just don't pay attention to me." he replied.

"Well, it's not all going to be easy, but we'll get there, sometimes they don't pay attention to me, either. Is there anyone I should talk to specifically?" I asked.

"No, not now." Jake answered.

"Remember what I told you," I said, "I will talk to Scouts who are having problems, that's my job. Most of the time things will work out, but when you need me don't be afraid to ask."

Jake looked at his cell phone, "Time for patrol meetings, excuse me," and he headed to the middle of the room to move things along.

A little later, I stood in the equipment room with our new quartermaster, three patrol quartermasters and a grumpy gear guru.

"Alex and Mr. Borgatti will help you three guys put together what your patrol needs for our next camping trip." I began, "Everyone have their cards?"

The three patrol quartermasters each held up an index card.

"Alex will take those, and hold on to them for you until next week. You guys can go join in the game now, and next week you'll come in here and sort out your patrol gear. I need to spend a little time with Mr. Borgatti and the quartermaster."

"So here's the plan." I said once the patrol quartermasters had left, "Next week Alex will meet with the patrol quartermasters and go over each thing on their list." I turned to Alex, "as you go over each list item they'll check the gear to make sure everything is there and ready to go, and then you'll set it aside so it can be loaded up Friday night. Got that Alex?"

"Sure, sounds easy enough," Alex replied.

"Work for you Rob?" I asked.

"I don't know why we have to go through all this," he shot back, "usually I just put things in the truck and we go, what's wrong with that?"

"Thanks, Alex," I said, "I want to talk with Mr. Borgatti for a moment; you can go back to the troop."

I turned to Rob, "I am trying to get the Scouts involved in the whole process. It will be fun for them, and they'll learn a few things too."

Rob looked at the ceiling, "You know we tried all of that before, years ago." he glared at me, "Scouts forget things, they break things, they lose things; that's why I do what I do. It's a lot easier and cheaper, by the way."

"If this was about going camping in the most efficient and easiest way possible, I'd agree with you, but that's not our goal." I began, "I want our Scouts doing more things for themselves. It may take some more effort on our part at first, but think about what they'll be learning as a result."

Rob ran his hand over his head and said, "Well, then, I'm out! I have this all figured, I've been doing it this way for years and no one complained."

Not what I was hoping for at all.

"I am sorry if you feel that I am complaining, Rob." I said, "All I am asking is that we get the Scouts involved, I am certainly not trying to criticize the job you've done."

"Well, I have had it! I'll call Mark and tell him," Rob pushed past me on his way out the door, "good night."

Two weeks in and one volunteer down; I wonder if that's a new Scoutmaster record?

CHAPTER NINE
Fifth Troop Meeting

What we need, and what, thank God, we've got in most places in our movement, is not merely the spirit of good-natured tolerance but of watchful sympathy and readiness to help one another. We not only need it but we've "got to have it" if we are going to teach our boys by the only sound way, that is through our own example, that greatest of principles — goodwill and co-operation.

B-P's Outlook

My committee chair called the next day, "Rob Borgatti was awfully upset, he says you were complaining about what he's done for us and bossing him around, I am afraid he's really quit this time."

"Well, Mark," I sighed, "I don't know what to tell you other than what I've already said. I am sorry to lose Rob's help, but if that's the way he feels I can't do much about it."

"Who is going to transport all of the troop gear if we don't have Rob's Truck? This is a disaster!" Mark moaned.

"I'll talk to Dave Stanley, he has a truck." I replied.

"After all those years, though, Rob's been around longer than I have." Mark went on, "Frankly Chuck, this is very upsetting; I hope we know what we're doing."

"I understand," I said, "The only thing I can say is I am proceeding as we agreed, Rob didn't like it, and I am sorry to see him go."

"I know, but let's not lose any more assistant Scoutmasters please?" Mark said.

"Dave, George, and Wayne have been very supportive, I think they are fine." I said.

"I'm going to give each of them a call," Mark said, "just to see how they take this."

"I'd appreciate it if you let me speak with them instead," I replied, "or at least let me speak with them first."

"Yeah, I suppose they are on your side of the organization chart." Mark said.

"That's what I was thinking," I said, "it's not about protecting my turf, but I think it's my responsibility."

"Yeah, that makes sense," Mark replied.

"Well, let's just be sure that you keep talking, and that we both understand each other." I said, "There are plenty of good things happening too." I went on to tell the committee chair about how well Jake and the patrol leaders were doing.

After I finished speaking to Mark, I called Dave, Wayne, and George to let them know Rob had resigned.

Our last meeting before the mountain climbing trip rolled around fast.

Dave Stanley appeared on cue about a half hour before the meeting,

"Dave, I really appreciate you doing this," I said shaking his hand.

"Well, what are assistant Scoutmasters for?" he smiled back.

"The whole thing's been a big upset," I said, "I was really taken by surprise."

"Didn't really surprise me that much," Dave replied, "Rob was always Rob, if you know what I mean. He and the last Scoutmaster were pretty good pals; I think it was just a matter of time, really."

"Well, I still feel bad about the whole thing," I sighed, "it's really been bothering me, and Mark is not too pleased, to put it mildly."

"Listen Chuck, I've been around a while, and I think I understand what you are trying to do." Dave said, "People come and go, it's to be expected, especially when some of the top roles in the troop change, don't take it too personally."

"I really appreciate that, Dave," I continued, "Can I tell you what I'd like to see happen so far as the gear goes?"

"I am all ears," Dave replied.

Dave and I spent the next few minutes going over my plan.

Jake was late getting to the meeting, so we had little time to talk, and one of his patrol leaders was home with a cold.

Things were getting kind of bumpy.

That evening the Scouts were loud, slow to follow directions, and this shook Jake's confidence.

"Everything okay Jake?" I asked.

"They aren't listening." Jake replied

"Who?" I asked.

"Zach and Hunter" he said, "they kind of think that because their dads are Scoutmasters they can do what they want."

"Would it help if I got involved?" I asked

Jakes face clouded, "Maybe, but..."

"But you don't want to be a tattle-tale?" I asked.

"Kind of," Jake said.

"I understand, Jake," I replied, "but it seems like getting me involved is kind of inevitable at this point. This is at least the second or third time you've mentioned this."

"Okay," he said, "I guess you should talk to them."

"I'll make a point of doing that as soon as I can." I said.

Because one patrol was leaderless, I met with them and tried to sort out their plans for the weekend. The patrol leader had whatever he had planned at home with him, and I was not very much help.

Mark, our committee chair, appeared without any notice and, while I was checking up on Dave and the quartermaster, took over the room to talk about climbing safety for ten minutes.

Somehow, we made it to the closing. As Jake reiterated our plans for the weekend, Mark interrupted him to go over permission slips, and I ended with a couple of disjointed thoughts in the guise of a Scoutmaster's minute.

I asked Zach, Hunter, and their fathers, George and Wayne, to speak with me briefly after the meeting closed. I told George and Wayne what was going on, and asked them to follow my lead.

"I wanted the five of us to discuss something, this shouldn't take long." I said, "George, I have been asking you to do a few things over the past couple of weeks, right?"

"Yes sir!" George said saluting.

"And you too Wayne?" I asked

"Yes." Wayne answered.

"And I appreciate how supportive and helpful you have both been," I said, "Why do you guys follow my directions?"

"Because you are the Scoutmaster, that's the way it works." Wayne answered.

I turned to their sons, "Zach and Hunter, if I gave you a direction you'd follow it, right?"

"Yeah," they replied.

"Whose directions is your senior patrol leader following when he asks you to do something?" I asked.

They looked at each other, "You, I guess," Zach said.

"That's right, he follows the Scoutmaster's directions and you Scouts elected him to be responsible for the good of the troop" I said, "I expect patrol leaders follow the senior patrol leader's directions as quickly as you'd follow mine. What point of the Scout law applies to what I am saying?"

Zach and Hunter thought for a moment.

"Obedient?" Hunter replied.

"That's right, good answer," I replied. "I'm glad you both understand, and the next time your senior patrol leader asks you to do something you'll get it done. Right?"

Zach and Hunter looked at me, not too sure what to do next.

"Can I get an answer to my question; the next time your senior patrol leader asks you to does something, what will you do?" I asked.

"What he says," Zach answered.

"Hunter?" I asked.

"What he says to do," Hunter replied.

"Thanks guys, I just wanted to be sure we understood each other' I said, "let me talk to your fathers for a minute."

Zach and Hunter headed out the door.

"Well," George said, "I'll talk to Zach about this."

"And I'll talk to Hunter." said Wayne.

"I think we made our point," I said, "so go easy, let's not make too much out of this."

"Yeah, but they have to understand how important this is," Wayne said.

"We are asking a lot from them, and from the other youth leaders right now, Jake was very reluctant for me to be involved," I said, "We can expect that things will be a little difficult for them at first; like I said, go easy."

We headed out the door; I locked the meeting room, stood in the parking lot for a moment and took a deep breath. If my first two weeks were steps forward, this one seemed like a step back.

CHAPTER TEN
On Our Way

Then the pitching of tents in separate sites and selected nooks, by Patrols … will give a keen interest and invaluable training.

B-P, *Aids to Scoutmastership*

"What happens when we get to the park?" I asked the Scouts as we drove to my first camping trip as their Scoutmaster.

Jake answered first, "Mm, I guess we set up tents?"

Jake, our senior patrol leader, was in the passenger seat. Our brand new quartermaster, Alex, was in the back seat with Bob, leader of the Fox patrol.

"Setting up tents is among the first few things, for sure," I said, "but think, step-by-step what happens when we pull into the parking lot."

"You put on the brakes, stop the car, and turn off the ignition!" said Bob from the back seat.

"That's a little more 'step by step' than I was thinking," I laughed, "but you're getting the right idea."

"I guess everybody gets out of the cars first?" Jake said.

"Then what happens?" I asked.

"We have to get our gear, right?" added Alex.

As we drove along we discussed each step along the way between pulling into the parking lot and getting into our tents for the night, and the Scouts formed a plan of action.

"Okay then, Jake, I'll show you and Alex the campsites," I reiterated, "Bob will get his patrol together along with the other patrol leaders, unload the cars, and then…"

"Everybody picks up their packs and I show them where their campsite is." said Jake.

"When we get there the first job is setting up tents." Bob continued, "I should be walking around making sure tents are getting set up, and helping when somebody needs me to."

"Bob," I said, "I am glad you remembered what we were talking about."

"No problem Mr. G!" he replied.

"That's important enough to go over one more time," I said, "if you are going to lead something like setting up tents, do your best to keep your head up looking around watching how things are going."

"Yeah, if you are concentrating on setting up a tent, I suppose it would be hard to get everybody else doing it." said Alex.

"That's the plan" I said, "what you'll learn, guys, is that you have to think two or three steps ahead of things to lead your Scouts, this weekend will be good practice."

"I made up the schedule for tomorrow like you asked," Jake said, "I hope it works."

"Your schedule is kind of like a map," I said, "and the day is like the terrain you are covering, does that make sense?" I asked.

"Yeah, I can see that," Jake replied.

"There's just one thing, though," I added, "you'll find out that the ground may be changing as you move along, something may take longer than you thought, or what you planned may have to change."

"Uh-huh," Jake said.

"How you respond when circumstances change your plans is what really makes a leader." I observed.

"The park is right down this road," I announced, "follow the plan you've come up with and we'll be fine."

We pulled into the parking lot. After Jake gave the patrol leaders some instructions, and I spoke with my assistant Scoutmasters, I led Jake and Alex down a trail nearby.

"You can put the third patrol over here," I said, "and the other two near the first and second fire rings we saw. The adults will all be up where we first came in. That's where you and Alex can set up too"

Jake and Alex nodded in agreement and we turned back, our headlamps lighting the way along the trail towards the parking lot.

Scouts were milling around, camping gear was everywhere, and as I approached, I heard a familiar voice, "Okay, so get your backpacks and we'll follow them, Scouts! SCOUTS!"

I quickened my pace a little and caught assistant Scoutmaster George Hudson in mid-bellow, "Mr. Hudson?"

"YES SIR!" George shouted as he delivered his comic salute.

"Mr. Hudson," I continued a little quieter, "the senior patrol leader knows what happens next, let's you and I walk over here."

"See that, you big galoot," said Wayne, another assistant Scoutmaster, as he followed us, "I told you he said to wait until he got back."

"Play nice now boys," quipped Dave Stanley, yet another assistant Scoutmaster leaning against his truck, "the boss is back, so play nice."

"I don't know who's worse," I said, "you three or the Scouts."

"Oh, definitely us," said George, "so what's going on?"

"Jake, Alex, and I scouted out the patrol campsites," I explained, "The Scouts are moving their packs down there now. They will be back up to grab their food and patrol gear, so let's help Dave empty his truck."

Alex, our quartermaster, appeared out of the darkness, "Are we ready yet?"

"I figure we'll make three piles of gear for each patrol," I explained, "and then you'll work with them to make sure they get all their stuff down to their campsites, sound good?"

"Sure," Alex replied.

"Remember, Mr. Quartermaster, I am expecting you to keep an eye on all of this gear," Dave said to Alex, "you have a big job to do this weekend."

"Right, Mr. Stanley." Alex replied.

"Oh, so now I see," George said, "Dave's your favorite, he can talk to Scouts but I can't huh?"

"Exactly," I replied, "a little more lifting, a little less talking Mr. Hudson, there's a truck to unload."

George saluted, "Yes SIR!"

Within an hour or so, the campsites were set up, and I had the adults sitting around our campfire.

"Jeez, how far away are those guys," Wayne asked nobody in particular.

"Close enough to keep track of them, but far enough to keep your nose out of their business." I replied.

"Sitting here just watching is turning out to be a lot more difficult than I thought," said George, "and that's odd because, usually, I like to sit around doing nothing."

"I am a little worried too," added Wayne, "I hope they figure things out."

"After last Monday, I'm happy we got here at all," I said, "things kind of got off track, didn't they?"

"That's not too unusual," Dave said with a smile, "it's never easy to begin with, and it's never all that simple, huh?"

"Tell me about it." I replied.

At that moment, we saw lights bobbing toward us and heard the thrashing of leaves as the Scouts came up from their sites. Soon they had gathered around our campfire.

"Jake, is everybody here?" I asked.

Jake started counting heads.

"Jake?" I whispered.

"Yeah?" he replied.

"You have patrol leaders?" I said quietly.

"Oh yeah," he smiled, "Almost forgot, Patrol leaders is everyone in your patrol here?"

"Rabbit Patrol?"

"Yep"

"Fox Patrol?"

"What? Oh, two, three, four, five… yes!"

"Hunter Patrol?"

"Yes sir!"

"Jake may I talk to everyone for a minute?" I asked.

"Sure," he replied, "Hey guys, quite down for a minute. Mr. Grant?"

"Thanks, Jake." I began, "As you know each patrol has a campsite all to yourselves, and that means you are being trusted, and that's something I want to talk about. What's the difference between a boy and a Scout?"

The Scouts all answered at once, and somewhere in there, I heard what I was looking for.

"Who said 'the Scout Law'?" I asked, "Hunter, was that you?

"Yes!" Hunter replied.

"Well that's exactly what I was looking for! Thank you! What's the first point of the Scout law Hunter?"

"Trustworthy!" he said.

"Exactly, because a Scout can be trusted. I know I can trust each of you because you are Scouts. I know that I don't have to worry that you'll misbehave because… anybody?"

Max answered hesitatingly, "We're Scouts?"

"Precisely, Max! I don't have to be concerned that you'll disobey your senior patrol leader or patrol leaders because…"

Several Scouts answered this time, "We're Scouts!"

"That's more like it," I was getting somewhere, "I didn't go camping with just a rag-tag bunch of boys this weekend, because…"

"WE'RE SCOUTS!" They all replied.

CHAPTER ELEVEN
First Night Camping

A week of camping is worth six months of theoretical teaching in the meeting room.

B-P, *Aids to Scoutmastership*

"Jake," I asked, turning to our senior patrol leader, "what time is lights out and all quiet tonight?"

Jake looked at his cell phone, "It's 9:45, what time do we have to get up in the morning?"

"Sounds like an excellent question for the patrol leaders' council," I replied, "why don't you send the Scouts off to their campsites, get your patrol leaders' council together, make a few decisions about times, and come talk to me when you are done."

"Right," Jake replied.

I dropped into my chair as the Scouts ambled down the hill toward their campsites.

"So far so good," said George, "I am beginning to think some of this may work."

"I don't know," said Wayne, "we haven't seen breakfast yet."

"Speaking of which," I said, "who's cooking our breakfast? I brought bacon and eggs."

"That'll be me, if that's okay," Dave said, "I am kind of itching to cook over a fire,"

"Sounds good to me," I replied.

Jake stepped into the firelight, "ten o'clock for lights out and all quiet, and we are getting up at seven."

"Okay, Jake," I replied, "like we talked about on the drive here, you've got your alarm clock and we'll call you when Mr. Stanley has your breakfast ready. Anything else?"

"You said the climbing guy is coming at ten tomorrow morning?" he asked, looking at his schedule.

"Yes, and it's about five minutes' walk from here to the rocks," I replied,

"The schedule is climbing for a couple of hours after breakfast," Jake said, "head back for lunch, and climb some more during the afternoon."

"Sounds good to me," I replied, "are you going to look in on the patrols before you go to bed?"

"Sure, I can do that." Jake replied.

"Sounds good, Jake," I said, "and thanks for all your hard work this evening.

"Okay, goodnight then." Jake said as he started down the hill.

Dave called after him, "Jake?"

"Yeah" Jake replied.

"Nice job this evening, you are turning out to be a pretty good senior patrol leader." Dave said.

"Yeah, what he said," Wayne added.

George chimed in, "He's right, Jake, good job."

"Thanks," Jake said, and went to check on his patrols.

I sat and talked with Dave, George, and Wayne as the fire turned into a glowing bed of coals.

"Have any of us actually looked at how the tents are set up?" Dave asked.

"Some of our newer Scouts haven't had much practice pitching tents." Wayne said.

"Or cooking," George added.

"I wonder if they remembered the ground cloths." Dave said to himself.

"I hope they put their food away properly," said George.

"I can think of ten or twelve things that may not be perfect right now," I answered, "but we aren't looking for perfection, just initiative."

"What if they really mess up something important though?" George asked.

"What happens if a Scout needs us, or something goes wrong overnight?" Wayne asked, "We are kind of spread out here."

"The farthest tent is really only about 25 yards away," I said, "I'll leave a lantern on so the Scouts can see where we are."

"If the lantern batteries run out," Wayne said, "they can always follow George's snoring."

"It keeps the bears away too," George said.

"There aren't any bears around here," Wayne replied.

"See how well that works?" George said, "I live to serve."

We sat and talked for a while longer as, one by one, lights in the Scouts tents went out.

"I have to cook breakfast," Dave said looking at his watch, "I think I'll turn in."

George stretched, yawned and said "Me too."

"I'm going to take a quick walk past the patrol sites," I said.

"Want some company?" Wayne asked.

"Sure, let's go." I replied.

We heard low talking in a couple of tents as we surveyed the campsites.

Wayne and I headed up the hill to our tents. "You know, they did a reasonable job of setting things up." he remarked.

"I saw a couple of things lying around but, all in all, so far so good." I replied.

"So far so good yourself, Chuck," Wayne said, "I'm still a little skeptical about the Scouts running things, but 'so far so good.'"

"That's pretty high praise from a skeptic" I replied, "I'll take what I can get!"

CHAPTER TWELVE
First Day Camping

In Scouting we know that what appeals to the boys, and is at the same time an education for them, is real camping.

B-P, Aids to Scoutmastership

Four Scouts huddled around the campfire circle in their patrol campsite.

A disorganized pile of leaves, grass, twigs and sticks and a bit of smoldering toilet paper lay in the campfire circle, along with a dozen burnt kitchen matches.

"How's it going?" I asked looking at the bowl of pancake mix waiting nearby.

Bob, their patrol leader looked up at me, "Not so great."

"I told you it wouldn't work, we need more paper." Jim said glumly.

"Everything's damp," Bob said, "let's get more dry sticks."

"Anybody have a pocketknife?" I asked.

Jim reached into his jacket pocket, pulled out a knife and held it up.

"Anybody try seeing if the inside of those sticks are dry?" I asked.

Four Scouts stared back at me like cats looking in a mirror.

"What happens if you open that pocket knife and split one of the sticks?" I asked, "Has anyone got a Scout Handbook?"

"Can we tear some pages out to start the fire?" Bob asked half seriously.

"I wouldn't recommend that" I replied laughing, "but I'll bet you'll have a fire pretty quickly if you take some advice from the handbook. You won't need any paper, either."

Eric got up from the circle and started rummaging around in a nearby tent for his handbook.

"I'll check back with you in a while, let me know if you need anything else." I said as I walked away.

I met George as he walked over from his son's patrol campsite.

"Well?" I asked.

George looked a little pale, "Not a total disaster, but close."

"They're eating something, though, right?" I asked.

"I detected a substance reputed to be oatmeal," he said, "if you are hungry enough you'll eat anything I suppose."

George and I started up the hill toward our campsite, "Jake, when you have a moment come see me." I called.

Dave and Wayne were washing up after breakfast, and Wayne's son Hunter was sitting by the fire.

"Hey Hunter," I said.

"Good morning Mr. Grant," he replied.

"How was breakfast?" I asked.

"Okay," Hunter said.

"Where's your patrol?" I asked.

"Huh?" he asked.

"Where's your patrol?" I repeated.

"Down there," he said pointing down the hill.

"And where should you be?" I asked.

"What?" he asked.

"And where should you be?" I repeated.

Hunter looked at his dad, looked at me, and said "With my patrol?"

"See, I knew you'd get it," I said, "see you later on."

"I needed to get something from my dad…," he said.

"Okay, now it's time to head back to your patrol, see you later." I replied.

Hunter looked at his dad, got up from the chair slowly, and started dragging his feet down the hill.

As soon as he was out of earshot, Wayne looked at me and said, "Thanks, he seems a little glum today. I didn't have the heart to get on his case, but thanks for doing that."

"No worries," I said, "anything in particular got him down?"

"Who can tell?" Wayne laughed, "He's thirteen!"

Dave laughed hard, "My son wanted to quit Scouts about two weeks out of four at that age. Of course the other two weeks he was having the time of his life."

Jake walked into the campsite, "You wanted to see me?" he asked.

"How are the patrols doing? Is everyone cleaning up after breakfast?" I asked.

"Well, the Rabbits are still cooking pancakes, The Hunter patrol is almost finished eating, and the Foxes are moving kind of slow." He answered.

"It's about 8:30," I said looking at my watch, "I expect to see our climbing guy in about an hour and a half, can I make a suggestion?"

"Sure," Jake said.

"First off, things are going pretty well," I began, "but as I was walking around this morning I saw a couple of things you may want to think about."

I went on to discuss a few minor things in the campsites that I thought could be improved. There was some gear laying around, one or two tents needed to be tidied up and staked better. We also talked through how dishes should be washed, fires doused, and food stored away.

"Your biggest challenge right now is working through your patrol leaders. You can't be responsible for every detail, that's why we have patrol leaders, right?" I asked Jake.

"Yeah, they are catching on, and they are at least listening to me most of the time." Jake said.

"So my talking with them helped?" I asked.

"Yeah." Jake said.

"Well, you are doing a great job," I said, "When you treat people with respect you get respect in return."

"Thanks," Jake said.

Dave Stanley handed Jake something wrapped in paper toweling, "Do me a favor, try this little invention of mine: a bacon, egg, cheese, and toast sandwich. You didn't eat more than two eggs and four or five pieces of bacon at breakfast."

"Nice!" Jake exclaimed, as he unwrapped the sandwich and took a big bite, "thanks Mr. Stanley!"

"Mr. Hudson?" Jake said through a mouthful of sandwich, as he walked away, "Zach said he needed to talk to you."

George looked up. Before he could answer I said, "Tell Zach Mr. Hudson is busy, he'll see him when we get together to go climbing."

"Murmph!" replied Jake as he continued down the hill.

"What if he really needs something?" George asked, a little worry creeping into his voice.

"If it was an emergency we'd run right down there," I replied looking into the Fox Patrol campsite, "I don't see anything that needs our attention from here."

"If he goes home and complains to his mother I am a dead man," George said, "maybe I should just…"

"DAD?" Hunter yelled from his campsite ten yards away. Wayne jumped, but before he could answer, I held up my hand, "Wait! Watch what happens next."

Jake stopped, turned and made a beeline for Hunter. Hunter and Jake talked for a moment and walked toward the Hunter patrol's kitchen setup.

"See that?" I said, "crisis diverted!'

Wayne and George exchanged concerned looks, and then looked at me, "Okay," Wayne said, "I get it, I think," he said with a smile.

George was still peering off toward the patrols, "I guess, I think I get it, maybe, but if he loses an arm and his mother finds out…"

"These boys," Dave began, "excuse me, these Scouts are used to having lots of adult 'help'; it's going to be a while before everyone gets comfortable with them doing for themselves."

"I guess it will take time for all of us to sort this out," George muttered.

"In the meantime," he turned to Dave, smiled, and asked, "professor, what is this amazing sandwich invention you speak of?"

CHAPTER THIRTEEN
Burnt Pancakes

We are not a club, nor a Sunday school, but a school of the woods.

B-P, *Aids to Scoutmastership*

"This one got kind of burny," Bob said, explaining the black pancake on his plate, "but it's eatable."

"How did the others turn out?" I asked.

"They were better after I had some practice," He replied.

"That's right," George said, "practice makes perfect."

George, Wayne and I strolled out of the patrol campsite.

"Looks like everyone has finished cooking and starting to clean up," I said, looking around.

"Yeah, and it only took two hours!" said Wayne looking at his watch.

"We won't win any prizes for speed," I laughed, "but they managed pretty well."

"How long did it take for the Rabbit Patrol to get a fire lit?" George asked.

"They were having trouble getting things going weren't they?" I said, "Whoever said 'where there's smoke there's fire' was apparently not a Scoutmaster."

"More like tortoises than rabbits," George quipped.

"Yeah, but remember who won the race!" I replied.

Jake caught up with us, "Mr. G!" he said, and "I think the climbing guy is here!"

"Looks like it," I replied looking towards the parking lot, "let's go meet him."

"Hey Mike," I said as we approached, "thanks so much for taking the time to help us out."

"Any excuse to do a little climbing," Mike replied taking my hand.

"This is Jake, our senior patrol leader," I said, "You'll want to work with him and figure out how we are going to make this happen."

"Sound's good," Mike replied, "Hi Jake."

"Jake," I said, "this is Mr. Carrigan."

Jake and Mike shook hands and the three of us discussed our plans for the day.

"Okay, Jake," I said, "you'll be leading things from here, any questions?"

"So we head for the rocks after the campsites are cleaned up?" he asked.

"Yup," I replied, "do you want the Scouts to bring anything with them?"

"I'll tell them to bring water bottles." Jake looked at Mike, "Anything else?"

"I'd like some help carrying this gear over," Mike told him, "but that's about it."

"I'll let you sort things out from here," I said, "I'll be around if you have any questions. Thanks again, Mike."

"Do *we* get to try climbing?" Wayne asked when I walked into our campsite.

"Sure, we'll let the Scouts go first," I advised; "let's hang back and see how things go."

Jake was making the rounds of the patrol campsites, soon the Scouts were headed up the hill and were milling around nearby.

"I think we're ready to go," Jake said.

"Good deal," I replied; "Any questions?"

"No, I don't think so," Jake said.

"Why don't you introduce Mr. Carrigan to everyone and head out," I asked; "we'll follow you over to the rocks."

We watched as the Scouts headed towards the parking lot, Jake made his introductions. Mike got a few Scouts to help him carry gear, and they headed down the trail toward the rocks.

"So far so good," George said, "It's sort of like being on safari, watching the wildlife in the distance."

"Grab your binoculars and your safari hat," Wayne said, "and we'll follow the trail of the wild Scout."

CHAPTER FOURTEEN
Second Night Camping

It is in the camp that the Scoutmaster really has his opportunity. He can enthuse his boys with the spirit that is required; the spirit is everything. Once that is developed, everything comes easy; without it, success in training the boys is practically impossible.

B-P's Outlook

"I think I am going to sleep pretty well tonight," George said through a yawn, "apparently I am not a natural-born climber."

"Men of a certain age and averdupois like us are creatures of the earth, not the air," I added, "I believe we all will sleep pretty well."

"What he said," Wayne chimed in, as he caught George's yawn.

Lights came bobbing up the hill toward us from the patrol campsites; soon a bunch of tired Scouts distributed themselves around the campfire.

Jake, our senior patrol leader asked each of the three patrol leaders if everyone was there, turned to me and said "looks like we are all here."

"Thanks Jake," I said, and turned to the Scouts, "we all had a pretty busy day, and I am certainly impressed with your climbing skills, but I am even more impressed with how far you have come as patrols in so short a time. Just think about what you did, you set up your own campsites, you cooked breakfast, lunch, and dinner..."

"Such as it was," George added under his breath.

I cleared my throat dramatically, and went on, "you got yourselves over to the rocks, learned something about climbing..."

"That was cool!" said a Scout, and others joined in with their comments.

"...and got yourselves back here; and soon," I continued, "you'll get a great night's sleep. Before we head off to bed, though, I asked Jake to bring you all up here so we could look over the day and see what we did well, and what we may be able to do better in the future. Let's start with you Jake, what did we do well?"

For the next few minutes the Scouts discussed their day, burnt pancakes, the challenges of "mountain" climbing, arguing over who washed dishes, all of the hundred things, large and small, about camping with their patrols.

"I want to say something," Hunter, patrol leader of the Hunter patrol, interjected, "It was pretty hard to be a patrol leader this morning, but we got better during the day, we did a lot that we haven't done before, and that was a good feeling, but I am really tired."

Hunter's father, Wayne, looked at me wide-eyed with amazement.

"I am glad to hear that Hunter," I said, "from what I have overheard I think a lot of you feel the same way," the Scouts murmured their agreement.

Zach Hudson's hand went up.

"Question Zach?" I asked.

"Yeah, do we get a badge for this?" he asked.

Dave Stanley stepped forward and looked at me, "I can answer that one if I may," I nodded and he continued, "like the counselor said today you've done a few things toward the climbing merit badge, and you can contact him if you want to complete the badge. So, Zach, part of the answer is no, you don't get a badge for today." Dave continued, "But if you think about the things you did today, I'll bet a lot of them would go toward meeting a few rank requirements."

"Today you did what Scouts do," I added, "and that always means you have done something toward your next rank, that's how it works."

Scouts looked at each other and whispered back and forth.

"Jake has some things to tell you about tomorrow morning before you head off to bed," I said, "Jake?"

I started walking away from the campfire, and motioned the three other adults to follow. We huddled a few feet away for a moment.

"So far so good," said George.

"This may, and I am just saying 'may', work yet," added Wayne; "I have no idea what happened to my son, but so far so good!"

"Yeah, how about that?" I said.

"Mr. Grant," Jake called, "I'm done,"

I led the adults back to the campfire.

"I want to say, once again, how proud we all are of what you all accomplished today. You have some great patrols, and patrol leaders, and chose a great senior patrol leader, thanks Jake!" I said, and shook Jake's hand as the Scouts applauded.

"Anything else for the good of the cause?" I asked turning to my assistant Scoutmasters.

Wayne began, "Great job Jake, great job boys…"

George broke in, "Excuse me, please, Mr. Murray; not 'boys'," George turned to the Scouts, "because…?" George waited expectantly, but no reply came, "C'mon guys! Back me up here? BECAUSE…?"

The troop caught on this time, and shouted back, "WE'RE SCOUTS!"

CHAPTER FIFTEEN
Blindsided!

Don't expect your life to be a bed of roses; there would be no fun in it if it were.

B-P, Aids to Scoutmastership

The last Scout hoisted his pack into the trunk of a waiting car, "Thanks Mr. Grant, Mr. Stanley; see you later!"

"Sure thing Jason," I replied, "see you soon."

"Well, Mister Scoutmaster, one down!" Dave smiled as he shook my hand, "and hopefully many more to go."

"Thanks Dave," I replied, "I was pretty happy with the way things went."

"I think the boys..." Dave stopped himself, "excuse me; I think the *Scouts* had a good time."

"I think they did," I replied, "burnt pancakes and all."

"They'll get better at things like that," Dave replied, "I, for one, am glad to see them finally get some practice."

"That's the idea," I said stifling a yawn, "I don't think anybody starved, and they all came back alive."

With that, Dave hopped in his truck, waved goodbye, and we both headed for home.

My wife woke me from a nap later that afternoon, handing me the phone, "its Cheryl, Bob's mother," she said.

I held my hand over the phone, "What's up?" I whispered.

"She says Bob is upset about something one of the other boys did," Anne whispered back, "apparently there was a fight?"

"Not that I saw," I replied, "any chance you want to figure this out?"

"Not on your life," she smiled, "this one is all yours."

"Hello Cheryl," I said, "this is Chuck."

"Hello Chuck," she replied, "Bob says that one of the other boys, Jason, hit him this weekend; he has a bruise."

"I'm sorry, Cheryl," I replied, "This is the first I have heard about it."

"I have already talked to Jason's father, who, may I say, is not a particularly polite man," she went on.

"Uh-huh" I said.

"I think Jason ought to be punished," Cheryl continued, "you know as well as I do he makes trouble at school, and I don't think my son should have to put up with this."

"Well, I can certainly understand how upsetting something like this can be." I said "Anne would be beside herself if our son…."

"How are these boys supervised?" she demanded, "Bob tells me that no adults were around when this happened, what was going on this weekend?"

"I don't think you and I are going to find many useful resolutions to all of this over the telephone," I said, "Let's get everyone together tomorrow night at the troop meeting and see if we can figure things out."

"I am not going to allow my son to be treated this way," she insisted; "This is assault, you know, I have half a mind to call the police."

"Can you come and meet with me tomorrow evening?" I asked, "I think that would be the best way forward."

"Yes, I'll be there," she replied, "I want that other boy punished, and I don't want him around my son."

"I understand; let's all get together and see what we can figure out. We'll talk tomorrow evening," I said; "sorry that this is so upsetting."

"Well," she retorted, "you have no idea how upsetting this is."

Once I had unsuccessfully tried to calm Cheryl down, I called Jason's home, and asked his father to come with Jason to our troop meeting. He said he understood, and would be there.

The third call was to my committee chair, Mark, so he could join us.

It was only Sunday, and I had already used up my "hour a week"!

CHAPTER SIXTEEN
Parents and Scouts

It is the spirit within, not the veneer without that does it. And the spirit is there in every boy when you get him, only it has to be discovered and brought to light.

B-P, *Aids to Scoutmastership*

The next evening, Dave and I sat at the picnic table with Jason and Bob, Mark was speaking to Bob's mother Cheryl, and Jason's father was waiting nearby.

"The story I have," I began, "is that you, Jason, punched Bob this weekend. Do I have that right?"

Jason looked at the ground; Bob was examining the backs of his hands.

"Jason, I need to hear from you." I said.

"He was bossing me around, he hit me, and I didn't like it." Jason said.

"Is that true Bob?" I asked.

"He wasn't listening to me," Bob replied, "so I tapped him on the shoulder, and then he punched me."

"Not 'tapped'," Jason said to Bob, "you hit me!"

"It was a tap," Bob said looking at me, "I didn't hit him."

"Why didn't you say anything to us this weekend?" Dave asked Bob.

"It wasn't a big deal." Bob said, "My mom saw the bruise when I got home and asked me how I got it."

"That explains a lot." I replied, "Obviously, Bob, this turned into a 'big deal.' I am not saying you're at fault, but we could have handled things better if we had known what was going on at the time."

"Yeah," Bob replied.

"So lesson learned," I went on, "next time someone, anyone, throws a punch or hits a fellow Scout I need to know."

"Got it," Bob said.

"Okay," I replied, "Bob, let me and Mr. S take a little time to talk to Jason, can you go wait over there?" I asked.

As Bob got up, I turned to Dave, "Can you ask Jason's father to join us?"

"Am I in trouble?" Jason asked.

"Well, let's get your dad over here and we'll all talk," I said.

I took a deep breath and closed my eyes for a moment; "so far so good," I hoped.

When Dave returned with Jason's father, I went over what Bob had said.

"Jason tends to over-react when he gets upset," his father said, "especially if he someone touches him. This is something we've been working on at School too; it's not an uncommon problem with autistic children."

"Can you tell me a little more about that?" I asked.

Jason's father went on to tell us that Jason had been diagnosed with mild autism in the second grade. Jason was able to keep up with his peers academically, but was having increasing difficulty with behavior after he entered middle school a month ago.

"Am I in trouble?" Jason asked again.

"Well, you did hit another Scout," I replied. "What do you think I ought to do about that?"

Jason looked away.

"Jason," his father said, "Mr. Grant is trying to help you, can you answer his question?"

"What question?" Jason replied angrily.

"You hit another Scout, and you hurt him," I repeated, "and I asked what you think I should do now."

"I don't like Scouts anymore." Jason said.

"Well," I replied, "do you think you should apologize to Bob?"

"He hit me first!" Jason said.

"I know that's what it felt like," I replied; "Did Bob tell you he was sorry?"

"No, he called me a swear after I punched him back," Jason alleged.

"Sounds like you were both angry," I said; "we all get angry sometimes."

Jason stared at the ground.

"Jason," I asked, "how can we help you find better ways to behave in Scouts?"

"Sometimes everybody just needs to leave me alone," he said, "sometimes I know when I have to stop, and I just can't."

"Okay, that makes sense," I said, "let's get Bob back here for a minute."

When Bob returned to the table, I asked Jason and his father to talk to him about what we had discussed.

"So if you need to get away from everybody," Bob asked, "we should just let you alone?"

"Yes," Jason replied, "my counselor at school says if I get upset I should walk away from everything; it helps."

"I understand that advice, Jason," Dave said; "But we want to make sure everyone is safe. We can't have Scouts running off alone, that's why we have the buddy system."

"Well, let's be sure that we understand that," I replied. Bob, can you be Jason's buddy?"

"I guess I can," Bob answered.

"What I mean precisely, Bob," I explained, " is you are a couple of years older than Jason, and as a patrol leader you can help him know that you understand more about what he is dealing with. We just have to have an understanding that you two stick together."

"Yeah, I can do that," Bob replied.

"That work for you guys?" I asked Jason and his father.

"Yes," Jason said as his father nodded his head.

"So we are almost done," I said, "I think you both got angry, you both acted out..."

"I just tapped him, though," said Bob.

"What name did you call Jason after he punched you Bob?" I asked.

Bob looked away, "I guess I called him something."

"So you both acted out," I continued, "and I think all that's left is for you to apologize to each other."

Bob said, "Sorry Jason," and reached out his hand.

Jason mumbled, "Sorry," and shook Bob's hand.

"Okay, Bob and Jason," I said, "why don't you head back to your patrol inside."

CHAPTER SEVENTEEN
Resolution?

No need for us to get depressed over temporary set-backs or disappointments; these are bound to come from time to time. They are the salt that savors our progress; let us rise above them and look to the big import of what we are at.

B-P's Outlook

As the Scouts got up from the table I turned to Jason's father, "Have you met Cheryl yet?"

"We talked on the phone," he said.

"Cheryl, Mark?" I called, "Do you have a minute?"

I introduced everyone as Cheryl and Mark joined us.

I explained what we had discussed with the Scouts, and how we had resolved the problem.

"What happens if he hits my son again?" Cheryl asked, "I don't understand how you can all sit here and say it was okay for someone to hit my boy!"

"Nobody is saying that it was okay," I replied, "just that we've better understood the causes behind what happened."

"I'm pretty sure that Jason was getting upset, he walked away from what was upsetting him to try to calm down," Dave explained. "Bob called him, and Jason didn't respond so Bob tapped him on the shoulder, and Jason punched him."

"We've had a difficult month," Jason's father sighed. "Jason has actually hit me and his mother," he looked at Cheryl, "you can imagine how upsetting that was. We've learned what causes him to react that way, and all three of us are working through it."

"Forgive me for saying so," Cheryl said, "doesn't that make your son dangerous to be around?"

"I honestly don't think so; once we understood how he reacts to being touched we were able to work with him." Jason's father answered. "If anyone is at fault it's me for not mentioning this to you. Like I said, this just started happening this past month or so."

"Well," I replied, "I think we've got things figured out now; I appreciate everyone's help with this."

"In light of what we have discussed," Mark replied," I think we can consider things resolved. Does that work for you Cheryl?"

"I am still worried that Jason is dangerous," she replied, "and I am having second thoughts about my son being involved with him."

"Talking to Bob a moment ago he didn't seem to feel that Jason was dangerous." I replied, "I think the two of them will get along fine. Bob's a very understanding Scout, and Jason seems to like him."

"He really had a wonderful time camping this weekend," Jason's father said, "he couldn't stop talking about Bob, either; he really looks up to him."

We continued to talk for a while. While I can't say that Cheryl totally agreed with the way things were handled she was at least willing to see how things went from there on out.

I huddled with Mark and Dave afterwards.

"Well?" I asked, "How do you think that went?"

"I'm a little concerned about supervision," Mark said, "I just think your idea of having them camp some distance away like you did last weekend isn't going to work."

"I don't know as I agree, Mark," Dave said, " I don't think we could have prevented this from happening if those two Scouts were standing right in front of us."

"Jason's mother was ready to call the police!" Mark said, "We can't have that sort of thing. I don't think you can be so cavalier about supervising Scouts."

"Anne would have been as upset if our son came home with a bruise like Bob did," I said, "but you heard what was said just a moment ago. Jason and his family are working through some challenges; Cheryl seems to understand that, and I think we reached a workable resolution."

"Well, I want you to assure me that you'll be supervising Scouts a lot more closely; we just can't have things like this happening." Mark said.

"I know it's upsetting, Mark," Dave affirmed, "This isn't a precedent-setting event. If you trust my judgment I'll say again, we could have been standing right there and not been able to prevent this from happening."

"Admittedly I wasn't there, and I do trust your judgment," Mark replied, "but the whole thing worries me."

"I'd imagine that anyone working with boys this age will have things like this happen from time to time," I said. "Let me speak with the Scouts this evening; I have been giving some thought to this and I have a few things to say."

I stood in front of the troop when it was time for my Scoutmaster's minute later that evening.

"Before you head home tonight I want to thank you Scouts for being trustworthy this past weekend." I began, "Does anyone recognize that word, trustworthy?"

Jason's hand went up, "It's in the Scout law!" he said.

"That's right, it's the first point of the Scout law, thanks Jason." I continued, "If you'll look around you at your fellow Scouts you are looking at people you can depend on to be trustworthy, friendly, and kind. Every one of your fellow Scouts will encounter situations that challenge their promise to follow the Scout law. If you look a little wider at the adults in this room, I think they'd agree with me that, no matter how old you get, we all encounter those sorts of challenges every day. Isn't that right Mr. Hudson?"

"You're older than me, Chuck, so I'll take your word for it!" George laughed.

"Thanks, Mr. Hudson," I said when the laughter died down. "That's right, even old guys like me are still working on being good Scouts; it never stops. The important thing, Scouts, is that we all keep the Scout law in our minds and hearts. When any of us come up short, we respond with kindness and friendship, that's what Scouts do."

I held up the Scout sign, "Let's remind ourselves of what we are all aiming at, a Scout is..."

We closed our meeting by reciting the Scout law.

Driving home that evening I wondered if other Scoutmasters have "normal" weeks.

If so, I'd like one sometime soon.

CHAPTER EIGHTEEN
Assistant Scoutmasters Meet

A further way of discovering activities that will appeal to the boys is for the Scoutmaster to save his brains by using his ears

B-P, Aids to Scoutmastership

"The next step," I began, "Is getting ourselves out of the middle of troop meetings."

George, Dave, and Wayne were sitting around my dining room table. They looked at each other, and back at me.

"Exactly how are we in the 'middle' of a troop meeting?" Dave asked.

"Well," I responded, "We do all of the instructing, and I'd like to see our Scouts doing that."

Wayne laughed out loud, and George looked a little worried.

"How can they instruct what they don't know?" asked Dave. "I don't get it."

"Yeah," George said, "if we aren't instructing them how are they going to learn; it's like giving the inmates the keys to the asylum."

"I'd like to see us instruct the instructors, rather than do it all ourselves." I replied.

"You know," George said, "Every idea you come up with seems to make things more complicated. Why fix things that aren't broken?"

"Do you honestly think Scouts would be able to keep their skills up if we stepped back?" Wayne asked, "Because I just don't see it, they don't understand how important these things are.;

"If our aim was simply creating a bunch of highly skilled Scouts," I answered, "I'd agree with you, but I don't think that's the point."

"So what is the point, then?" asked Dave.

"What I'd like to focus on are Scouts who know how to learn, who develop some instructional and leadership skills," I replied, "rather than focus only on the quality of their skills, or how many requirements we can tick off the list."

"So they can just slide by? We don't have any standards?" George asked, "We really make sure they know their stuff; I'd hate to see us turn into a merit badge factory."

"I think," I answered, "we can have good skills, high standards, and Scouts who know how to learn nearly anything, without us being in the middle of it all."

Over the next few minutes, I laid out my plan, and managed to get my three assistant Scoutmasters to agree we could give it a try.

"So, let me get this straight," George said, "the Scoutmaster is the head coach, coordinating each of us, your assistant coaches, who look after some aspect of the game."

"Yes," I replied, "and 'game time' is at meetings and on camping trips."

"And during game time we stick to the sidelines," Wayne added, "makes sense to me."

"And to strain the metaphor a little further," I continued, "Our coaching time is mainly what happens when the patrol leaders' council gets together."

"What about cheerleaders?" George asked, "We get to have cheerleaders, right?"

"It's only a metaphor," I laughed, "let's not go too far with it."

"Yeah, George," Wayne said, "calm down."

"Just trying to get in the spirit of things," George replied.

CHAPTER NINETEEN
Patrol Leaders' Council

To an outsider Scouting must at first sight appear to be a very complex matter. But it need not be so, if the man will only realize the following points:

1. The aim of Scouting is quite a simple one.

2. The Scoutmaster gives to the boy the ambition and desire to learn for himself by suggesting to him activities which attract him, and which he pursues till he, by experience, does them aright.

3. The Scoutmaster works through his Patrol Leaders.

B-P, Aids to Scoutmastership

"I want to ask you a question," I began when our patrol leaders' council meeting rolled around, "What is your goal?"

"To have fun!" Bob piped up.

"To learn Scout stuff?" Hunter offered.

"To lead, I guess?" Jake said.

"I think those are all good answers," I replied, "How do we know that our Scouts are having fun, learning skills, and benefitting from your leadership?"

The Scouts looked back at me with furrowed brows.

"That's a tough question, isn't it?" I asked. "Was your mountain climbing trip fun?"

"Yeah," Jake replied, "that was fun, and I had a good time."

"*Very* fun," Zach added.

"Did you learn Scout stuff?" I prodded.

"I learned how to burn pancakes," Bob said.

"Yes, you did," I laughed, "and you fulfilled a couple of requirements for rank, too. Right?"

"Did I?" Bob looked puzzled.

"Yes," I answered, "and I'll look those over with you later if you like, Bob. Did the Scouts benefit from your leadership on the trip?"

"I think so," Hunter replied, "at least a little."

"I think you are selling yourself short, Hunter," I replied, "You guys did a great job."

"Thanks," Hunter replied.

"So we know that those things, fun, skills, and leadership are all big parts of your goal," I continued. "And we know that you achieved that goal on the weekend, but I am looking for more than that. What can we use as a goal that we can keep track of, so we know when we've reached it?"

The Scouts stared back, waiting.

"I'll give you a hint, it's in your Scout handbook, and you get a badge for it."

"Do you mean a rank or a merit badge or what?" Jake asked.

"Getting warmer, Jake," I smiled, "It's a rank."

"Eagle?" he asked.

"What do you have to do before Eagle?" I asked.

"Life?" Jake replied.

"Star!" Bob said.

"First Class?" added Hunter.

"Bingo, you win Hunter," I said, "First Class is important because once Scouts have reached it they have learned all the basic Scouting skills, right?"

"I suppose," said Jake, "seems right to me."

"So if your Scouts reach First Class," I said," that means you have done a lot for them, you've reached your goal."

"I get it, I think," said Zach.

"I think it's your job to lead, train, and inspire Scouts to reach First Class," I said, "does that make sense?"

"Sort of, "Jake replied, "but what about fun, though?"

"Bob's experience on the weekend is a good example," I answered, "he had fun cooking, and he fulfilled a requirement, too, right Bob?"

"Fun?" Bob mused, "It was hard, but fun I guess."

"So Bob was doing what Scouts do," I said "he was cooking, right?"

The Scouts nodded their heads.

"Doing what Scouts do is fun, and it gets you to First Class. See how it's all kind of connected?" I asked.

"Yeah, I think so," Jake said.

"Jake," I asked, "How do Scouts become First Class?

"By doing things that Scouts do?" he answered.

"Precisely," I said, "Hunter, what do Scouts do?"

"Burn pancakes," Hunter answered, and the Scouts laughed.

"So cooking?" I said smiling.

"Yeah, 'cooking,'" Hunter replied.

"What else?" I asked

So far so good. Over the next few minutes we had quite a list: camping, swimming, climbing, learning skills, pioneering, first aid, and lots more. As the Scouts named them, I wrote them on our whiteboard.

"Where do Scouts do all these things?" I asked.

"We do them at meetings sometimes," Bob answered.

"We did a lot on the weekend," Hunter added.

"So Scouts do what Scouts do by attending and being prepared to participate in the events we plan." I stated.

"Why do Scouts come to meetings and go camping?" I asked.

"To have fun," Bob answered.

"So now we are back at the beginning," I said, "because we already figured out what 'fun' is right?"

"Okay, wait," Jake began, "we have fun when we do what Scouts do, and we do that stuff at meetings and campouts, and when we do that stuff we get to First Class."

"Now you're talking, Jake!" I replied, "You've described it exactly. Let's see what that looks like."

I turned to the whiteboard in our meeting room and wrote;

Scouts have fun

by

Doing what Scouts do

at

Meetings and on Camping trips

and

They earn First Class

"Does that start to make sense now guys?" I asked.

The Scouts stared at the board for a while.

"Now I get it," Hunter said.

"So what's your job as a patrol leader Hunter?" I continued.

"I guess to get Scouts to do advancements?" Hunter replied.

"That's certainly part of it, but what's at the top of the list?" I asked, pointing at the board.

"Fun," Hunter said.

"And then?" I asked.

"Doing what Scouts do," Hunter answered.

"Where?" I continued.

"At meetings and campouts," Hunter said.

"Then what?" I prodded.

"They get First Class," Hunter replied.

"So I'll ask you again;" I said, "what's the patrol leader's job?"

"To have fun?" Hunter replied.

"Good," I said, "but let's remember you are leading the fun, right?"

The Scouts nodded.

"I said this a few minutes ago, let's write it down." Turning to the board, I wrote:

Lead, Train, and Inspire Scouts to become First Class.

"Remember that?" I said, "Your example and encouragement as leaders is the most important factor in making this happen."

I looked at my watch. Fifteen minutes had passed since we sat at the table.

"Jake," I asked the senior patrol leader, "I appreciate you letting me take some time to talk; I know you have some things to go over about the next four or five meetings. How about you do that now and I'll come back when you are done?"

"Okay Mr. G.," Jake replied as he rummaged around in his book bag.

Jake and I had spent some time talking and emailing back and forth the past week. He'd prepared a "to do" list for his patrol leaders that would guide them through planning the next few troop meetings.

I got up from the table and joined my three assistant Scoutmasters in our gear room.

CHAPTER TWENTY
With Assistant Scoutmasters

The Patrol System has also a great character-training value if it is used aright. It leads each boy to see that he has some individual responsibility for the good of his Patrol. It leads each Patrol to see that it has definite responsibility for the good of the Troop. Through it the Scoutmaster is able to pass on not only his instruction but his ideas as to the moral outlook of his Scouts.

B-P, Aids to Scoutmastership

"How's it going?" asked Dave when I stepped through the door of our gear room.

"Well," I replied, "they sat through fifteen minutes of me going on, but I think it was useful."

"So when do we get to go talk to the patrol leaders?" Wayne asked.

"Like we discussed the other night," I replied, "I'll ask you to come in for the last 20 minutes or so and get your assignments."

"Won't they need some help planning?" George asked.

I reiterated what we had discussed around my dining room table. "Jake and I have been working on this, and what needs to happen over the next few weeks. He has a plan, and he'll have things for all of us to do."

"I think that's a good idea," Dave said, "let's see what they come up with first."

"Sounds like you've already decided for them," Wayne objected, "How much of this is really Jake's idea and how much is yours?"

"Most of the framework is mine," I said, "but the execution of the plan is up to Jake. The first couple of times they go through this I will be more involved in setting things up. We are writing our playbook here; once the team practices the plays a few times they'll be able to call them on their own."

"But what if they've missed something?" Wayne asked.

"It's almost sure that they will," I said; "part of the process is letting them work this out, and to do that they need to miss things every once in a while."

"Okay, but if they miss something we can back them up?" George asked.

"Just how we go about doing that," I replied, "is going to be very important to developing independent leadership skills, so I'll ask that you follow my lead."

"Which means we can't say anything, right?" George remarked with an edge of frustration.

"That's pretty much it," I said, "I know this will be frustrating at first, but we are in this for the long haul."

"It's no good if we are all putting our oar in as much as we have in the past," Dave explained, "I guess we have to accept things may be a little disjointed for a while."

"But isn't it our responsibility to make sure that they are holding up their end of things?" Wayne asked.

"Yes, we'll keep an eye on that," I answered, "but we'll only step in if there's a safety issue, how about that?"

"So you aren't worried that the whole program can just crash and burn?" said George.

"I doubt we'll have literal flaming wreckage," I replied smiling; "let's remember that they managed very well on the camping trip."

"Okay," George stated, "I'll give you that; but I still think this whole thing is shaky."

"There's no doubt," I observed, "that we are better instructors, better planners and better leaders; but we only developed those skills by practice, and some trial and error. We made mistakes, we forgot things. When we step back our Scouts can develop those skills the same way."

"They did buy and cook their own food last weekend," Dave said, "and we weren't too sure they would be able to do that."

"That's right," George said, "I guess I just worry that these big changes are happening too fast."

"At some point, though," I said, "we have to let go of the bikes and let each of them ride on their own."

"So long as they have helmets on," George said.

"Yeah, and training wheels," Wayne added, "and maybe baseball cards in the spokes, those are cool."

"There goes my metaphor," I laughed, "strained to the breaking point again. Let me get back to the patrol leaders' meeting and I'll call you guys in in a few minutes."

When I returned to the patrol leaders' council Jake reviewed their plans for the next month.

"The next camping trip is backpacking," Jake said, "and we'll be hiking on the blue trail at Catamount; that's about seven miles."

"What do you have planned for your meetings?" I asked.

"Next week we'll do cooking," Jake replied, "but the kind of cooking you need for backpacking, and that's different."

"Before you go on, let me ask you a couple of questions," I said, "who is going to instruct the Scouts?"

"We were going to ask Mr. Hudson," Jake said. "He does cooking merit badge."

"How about one of you guys doing the instructing?" I asked.

Jake looked puzzled. "Won't Mr. Hudson be there?"

"So far as I know he will," I answered, "but I'd really like to have a Scout instruct rather than an adult, who'd like to give it a shot?"

"I like cooking," Alex, our quartermaster, replied, "I could try."

"Would that be okay with you Jake?" I asked.

"Sure, I guess so," Jake answered.

We spent the next few minutes going over the rest of the meeting plans for the month and sorting out who would be doing what.

I called my assistant Scoutmasters to join us.

"Jake has some requests for you gentleman," I said, "Jake?"

"Mr. Hudson," Jake began, "works with Alex about cooking, Mr. Stanley works with Hunter about gear and packing, and Mr. Murray works with Zach about map and compass."

"So each of you," I said, "will pair up with a Scout and help them prepare to instruct those things. How long are the sessions Jake?"

"Ahhh," Jake looked at his notes, "thirty minutes at each of the next three meetings."

"And you and I will be working on what happens at patrol meetings and games, right?" I asked.

"That's the plan," Jake replied.

"Okay then," I said looking at my watch, "We have around TWENTY-minutes left. How about we pair up and start preparing?"

My "assistant coaches" were prepared, and headed off to work with their "special teams" while I discussed a few details with Jake, our "team captain."

So far so good.

CHAPTER TWENTY-ONE
Sixth Troop Meeting

But to get first-class results from the patrol system you have to give the boy leaders real free-handed responsibility - if you only give partial responsibility you will only get partial results. The main object is not so much saving the Scoutmaster trouble as to give responsibility to the boy, since this is the very best of all means for developing character.

B-P, Aids to Scoutmastership

A few minutes before our next troop meeting, Jake went over the plan as the patrol leaders huddled around. He turned to me and asked, "Anything else Mr. G.?"

"Sounds like you have things under control," I replied, "we'll be right here if you need us."

The Scouts headed towards the meeting room as I turned to my three assistant Scoutmasters.

"See, no big secrets, just a quick huddle," I noted.

"That was fast," George remarked.

"When *you* are only listening," Wayne said, "things go faster."

"That's the general idea," I replied, "I know it's a little different for you guys, but it works."

"We'll get a chance to see if it does or not," Dave added, "but so far so good."

"What I ask you all to do this evening," I emphasized, "is keep your distance and just observe what's happening."

"What if they need some help instructing?" George asked.

"Let's do our best not to say anything," I answered, "just let them play the game. We'll watch first, and save the talk for later."

"So no helping?" George continued.

"Only if asked; no jumping in." I replied, "If something really goes off the rails, and I am talking about unsafe or inappropriate actions, then step in. Otherwise just watch."

"I'll be in the gear room," Dave said, "that'll keep me out of trouble."

"I set up an observation post inside," I said, "a couple of chairs along the back wall, that's our spot if we are going to be in the room."

"You have got to be kidding me," George said. "Really?"

"Yeah, really!" I laughed, "Let's see how it works out. If it makes you nervous you can always help Dave in the gear room."

"Sir, yes sir!" George saluted, "Sir, it may drive me crazy, sir!"

"Well, if it does at least it will be a short trip," Wayne laughed.

George punched him in the arm.

From the "observation post", most of the meeting looked and sounded like a flock of geese landing, staying on the ground for a moment, and then taking flight again.

"At least they sound happy," George remarked, "but it sure is loud in here."

"I am getting dizzy," Wayne said.

Zach was working with a group of Scouts off in the far corner of the room.

"Look over there," Wayne pointed, "Zach and I worked on this, let's see how things go."

Zach had a compass in his hand, and was pointing out something on a map laid on the table. His group of Scouts were watching, talking, tussling, and squawking all at once.

A few minutes later Jake signaled and the Scouts dashed around the room to their next activity.

"Wow," George said, "I am getting dizzy too, things are so... so"

"Chaotic?" I asked.

"Yeah, it's like watching a school of fish." George said.

"Or a herd of cats," added Wayne.

"How about a colony of ants?" asked George.

"More like a hive of bees," laughed Wayne, "It's not *that* bad, though, I do see things happening."

"I think it's a trick of perspective," I mused, "I'll be interested in what the Scouts have to say."

While the Scouts played a game, I met with my assistant Scoutmasters.

"After the closing, the patrol leaders' council will meet, and then we'll have the opportunity to reflect with the Scouts we are each working with," I began. "What I'd like you to do is ask them how they thought things went, and offer one or two observations. Limit yourself to one or two, let's not overload them. Pick one improvement for next week, and work with them on that."

At the closing, Jake turned to me, "Your turn, Mr. G."

"Thanks Jake" I stepped in front of the Scouts, "who learned something this evening?"

About three fourths of Scouts raised a hand.

"What did you learn, Eric?" I asked turning to a young Scout.

"Compass stuff!" he said.

"Can you tell me one specific thing?" I asked Eric.

"Yeah, the bird points are south, east, north, and west." Eric replied.

"Bird points?" I asked.

"He means *cardinal* points," Zach corrected, "not bird points."

"Yeah, *cardinal*, like a bird." Eric said.

When the laughter died down I said, "I think you got the important part, good job Eric! You too Zach!"

The patrol leaders' council huddled round after the meeting closed.

"That's what happens next week," Jake said finishing up; he turned to me, "Mr. G.?"

"Thanks Jake," I began, "just a couple of quick questions, then I want you to meet with whoever you are working with on skill instruction next week. Did you guys think things went well this evening?"

"I think so," Bob replied.

"It was okay," Zach chimed in.

"Nobody listened to me," Hunter said.

"From what I saw," I said turning to Hunter, "you did a pretty good job getting through to them, though."

"I guess, but everybody was just talking and stuff," He replied.

"Maybe the answer is to be sure you have something active planned next time," I remarked, "do you think that would help?"

"Yeah, maybe," Hunter answered, "it was more like I was just talking to them and they wouldn't listen."

"Well, that's something to think about," I said, "I don't think Scouts come here to sit and listen; you guys would probably rather be doing things than listening to someone talk, right?"

The Scouts nodded their heads.

"And in that spirit, I am done," I concluded; "spend a few minutes working with the adult helping you and we'll all head home."

"So, honestly guys," I asked as I locked the meeting room door, "do you think the way we handled this meeting works for you?"

"We have a *looong* way to go," George said putting on his coat.

"We sure do!" I replied. "And once we arrive we'll start all over again."

"I think they are catching on," Wayne said, fumbling for his keys, "Zach and I talked about a couple of things; he seems to be excited about instructing."

"I gave Bob a couple of hints about crowd control," Dave added, "he was struggling with keeping everyone's attention."

"That's a big challenge," I said, "Naturally adults can run a more orderly meeting, we are better than Scouts at nearly everything."

"Except climbing," George laughed.

"And," Wayne added, "running around like a flock of chickens."

"Or a passel of chipmunks," George said.

"Or ten squirrels in a cardboard box," Wayne laughed.

"You two really need to be separated," I said. "Good, bad or indifferent, the important thing is that they did this for themselves."

"Yes, there is that," George replied. "I just worry about the level of skill, and how this approach affects them advancing."

"If things work as they are supposed to," I said, "we'll see them advance and gain some important skills, too."

"I can see that happening," Dave said; "you know, this is a pretty sharp bunch."

"Thanks everyone," I said, "I am headed home!"

"Home?" George replied, "What's that?"

"It's where your wife and children live." Wayne said.

"Right, I almost forgot!" George joked. "See you later!"

CHAPTER TWENTY-TWO
Second Committee Meeting

So, in dealing with the Scouts, you are bound to meet with disappointments and setbacks. Be patient: more people ruin their work or careers through want of patience than do so through drink or other vices. You will have to bear patiently with irritating criticisms and red tape bonds to some extent but your reward will come.

B-P, Aids to Scoutmastership

"Thanks for that report, Chuck," Mark said, "are there any questions for Chuck from the committee?"

I looked around the table at the committee members.

"I heard about a couple of Scouts fighting on the camping trip, what happened?" asked Barry, our membership.

"First of all it wasn't a fight; there was one punch thrown and some heated words exchanged. Mark and I spoke with the Scouts involved and their parents," I replied, "we resolved the issue a week or two ago."

"I think we should have a zero-tolerance policy on that sort of thing." Barry said, "We ought to suspend any Scout who gets in a fight."

"There should be some sort of consequences," Fran, our treasurer, added, "I know at least one of the boys involved is a constant problem in school."

"Let's take some time to discuss this," Mark said, "Chuck and I have talked about how we will respond to behavior problems, can you tell everyone a little about this, Chuck?"

"Whenever a Scout misbehaves my response is to counsel them." I answered, "Depending on the nature of the misbehavior, they will deal with any immediate consequences right then and there."

"Is that how you responded to the fight?" asked Barry.

"Before I answer that question, Barry, let me go on a bit." I answered, "Once I have counseled with the Scout I may choose to speak with his parents about the issue. They can respond to the problem at home as they see fit."

"So no punishment?" Barry persevered.

"It's not my role to punish Scouts," I replied, "that's their parents' prerogative. Like I said: Scouts who misbehave will deal with any immediate consequences of that misbehavior, like cleaning up a mess they made, or something similar."

"So how did you deal with the fight?" Barry asked.

"Let me jump in if that's okay," Mark said; I nodded, "As soon as we knew about the problem Chuck and I talked. Then we met with the Scouts and parents and resolved the issue."

"Well, I think the committee should know exactly who we are talking about and exactly what was done." Barry said, "I think we aren't being responsible otherwise."

"I understand your concern, Barry," Mark went on, "but we aren't going to discuss specifics about this kind of incident. If your son or my son was involved in something like this, I think we'd appreciate some sensitivity to making the issue a topic of general discussion."

"I don't agree," Barry replied, "couldn't we all end up getting sued for something like this?"

"I think you are overstating the case," Mark said, "Let's not make mountains out of molehills."

"Let me make sure I've understood you Chuck," Fran said, "you will ask parents to punish Scouts if you think it's needed?"

"I wouldn't ask them to punish their child," I replied, "that's not my place. I will talk with them about the incident, but what they choose to do about it at home is really no one else's business."

"What if a parent doesn't do anything?" asked Barry, "and the Scout keeps acting up?"

"At that point I will ask them to keep their son at home until they can assure me the behavior problem is solved." I replied.

"So you *are* suspending them?" Fran asked, "For how long?"

"I am not suspending them," I replied, "I am just telling parents that we can't have a Scout actively involved who routinely misbehaves in a serious manner. I leave it up to them how they will resolve that problem with their own child, and when they can assure me they have addressed the behavior we can have the Scout actively involved again."

"So how do you define 'serious' misbehavior?" Barry asked.

"Anything that is routinely disruptive, or presents a danger to their fellow Scouts," I replied.

"And we just leave this definition up to you?" Barry continued.

"Forgive me for interrupting," Mark said, "but I'll answer that question; Chuck and I will judge these issues as they come up, and if we feel that the committee needs to get involved, we'll certainly ask for your help."

"I'd like us to vote on that, because I don't agree," Barry said.

"Well, Barry, we've talked about this before. Our chartered organization chose me to chair the committee, and I chose our Scoutmaster with your advice and consent." Mark said, "This isn't subject to a vote, this is my decision."

"Why are we even here?" Barry continued, "If we don't have a say in the way things are done?"

"May I say something?" Roger, a long-serving committee member, asked.

"Certainly Roger," Mark replied, "I just ask you to be brief; we have a number of items on the agenda to discuss yet."

"I will be brief; thanks Mark," Roger began. "To answer your question Barry, we are here to help make things happen for our Scouts. Committees like ours are advisory, not democratic. While we do vote from time to time, these votes are a way of expressing consensus and support for ideas and directions."

"So the chair can do whatever he wants, then?" Barry asked.

"Yes, so long as his actions are in accordance with the policies and procedures of both our chartered partner and the national organization." Roger replied. "Should any members of the committee disagree with an action or decision by the chair, they can take it up with our chartered organization representative. Thankfully I don't recall this ever happening in the ten or fifteen years I have been involved with our troop."

"I have served on a number of committees, and none of them functioned like a dictatorship." Barry said.

"I wouldn't go so far as to call it a dictatorship," Roger smiled; "we usually overcome disagreements amicably. As Mark explained, he answers to the chartered organization representative and both of them are responsible for assuring we are presenting the Scouting program as written. I imagine if Mark answered to us we could end up redefining Scouting into something other than what it was intended to be."

"Well, I'd like to see where it's written that the Scoutmaster and committee chair can make decisions without the consent of the committee," Barry persisted.

"Thanks for your input Roger," Mark said. "In the interest of time, Barry, how about you, Chuck and I put our heads together after we are done here? We need to move on."

Mark continued with the agenda, and I left the meeting to consult my Scoutmaster's handbook.

After the meeting adjourned, Mark and I met with Barry. I showed him the Scoutmaster's job description in my handbook. In the end, he agreed that Mark and I did have the responsibilities we had discussed even if we weren't carrying them out exactly as he would.

Apparently getting everyone pulling in one direction takes more explaining and listening than I had anticipated.

I suppose it's all part of the job.

I even appreciate it when someone challenges what you are doing. When they do, it's an opportunity to be sure you are getting things right.

Even so, my first two committee meetings left me feeling a little ragged!

CHAPTER TWENTY-THREE
On the Trail

Here, then, lies the most important object in the Boy Scout training - to educate; not to instruct, mind you, but to educate, that is, to draw out the boy to learn for himself, of his own desire, the things that tend to build up character in him.

B-P, Aids to Scoutmastership

I took in the vista as I reached the overlook, shed my pack and plopped down on the rocks next to George.

"That was some climb, huh?" I said, "But it was worth it."

"Beautiful spot," George replied looking past me, "Watch the edge there guys!"

Our Scouts were looking into the valley below from the edge of the rocky ridge.

"Jake," I called, "can I have a word?"

Jake bounded over the rocks, "What's up Mr. G.?"

"Everyone make it okay this morning?" I asked.

"So far so good," he replied, "It took a little longer than we thought, but apart from fixing a few packs along the way everybody did good."

"Mr. Hudson and I have one favor to ask," I said, "would you please be sure that the Scouts are being safe around that edge?"

"Sure," Jake said looking over his shoulder at the Scouts, "Hey Bob!" he shouted, "Tell Eric to get back, please!"

Bob stepped up to Eric, and they both moved back.

"No climbing around, please," I said to Jake, "keep your eyes open. You guys making lunch?"

"Yeah, I think so," Jake said.

"Thanks Jake," I said, "let us know when you are ready to go."

"No problem," Jake said as he returned to the group of Scouts.

"Our lunch," George said, "is in your pack, and here comes Dave."

Dave was only a few steps behind me on the trail, and he climbed up to sit with George and me.

The past few weeks had gone by quickly. Jake had done an admirable job of leading the patrols through the preparations for our backpacking trip.

At each of the four troop meetings leading up to the trip the patrol leaders' council had shared in instructing Scouts on some aspect of backpacking.

I smiled as I watched the Scouts busily opening packs and preparing their lunch in the warm autumn sunlight.

"I, for one, am impressed," Dave, said between sips of soup, "I honestly didn't think we'd get all the way here in time for lunch."

"They were pretty slow getting packed up this morning," George added, "but they made it."

"Hopefully they still have everything they started with last night." I laughed.

"We had to chase a loose sleeping bag down one of the switchbacks," George laughed, "I thought it might roll all the way to the bottom of the mountain!"

"I'll bet that sleeping bag is strapped on pretty tight now, though!" I said.

"I have to say, too, Chuck," said George, "you've almost made a believer out of me."

"Wow," I said, "that's encouraging."

"Zach has really perked up the past few weeks," George went on, "he's loving being a patrol leader, and he had his own pack packed last Wednesday."

"Well, what could be better than backpacking with your buddies?" I asked. "This has always been one of my favorite trips, too."

"Yeah, they are all having a good time," Dave said.

"From what I have seen, it looks like they are pretty well prepared, too." I added, "Nobody's mentioned having forgotten anything."

Zach drifted towards us as we ate our lunch.

"So what are the Rabbits having for lunch, Zach?" Dave asked.

"You mean Rabbit/Hunters?" answered Zach, "we have a couple of guys from the Hunter patrol with us because Hunter didn't come with us."

"Sorry, Zach," Dave laughed, "what's the Rabbit/Hunter patrol got for lunch?"

"Soup," Zach said, holding out his mug, "cheese, salami and pita bread."

"Sounds good," Dave said; "plenty for everyone?"

"So far so good," Zach answered.

"Hey Zach," George asked his son, "Where is your patrol?"

Zach gave his dad a playful scowl, "Alright, I get it, love you dad."

"Love you too son," George replied, "See you later."

"Well done!" I said patting George on the back.

"Yeah, I get it too, you know," George emphasized, "He needs to keep his eye on the ball."

A half hour or so later Jake came back where we were sitting, "I told everyone it was time to go; it's three miles to our campsite from here."

"Are you still hiking the point?" I asked.

"Yeah," Jake said, "the Foxes are behind me and the Rabbit-Hunter patrol is next, you still hiking the sweep position?"

"By aptitude more than choice," I laughed, "Mr. Stanley and I are still the slowest. Mr. Hudson will be toward the middle of the group I suppose?"

"Yep, I'll try to keep up," George assured us.

We hoisted our packs and headed over to join the Scouts.

"Here's where we are now," Jake said pointing out the ridge on his map, "and here's the campsite. We'll catch everyone up here, that's about halfway to the end."

"Who can get us started?" I asked the Scouts.

"Let me try!" Eric offered, as he fumbled around in his jacket for his compass.

"Okay, Eric," Jake said, "show me where we go."

CHAPTER TWENTY-FOUR
Hitting our Stride

It is the satisfaction of having successfully faced difficulties and borne pin-pricks that gives completeness to the pleasure of having overcome them.

The satisfaction which comes of having tried to do one's duty at the cost of self-denial, and of having developed characters in the boys which will give them a different status for life, brings such a reward as cannot well be set down in writing.

B-P, *Aids to Scoutmastership*

After four weekend outings and a couple dozen meetings, the changes I initiated early in the fall began to become routine. Four months into his term, Jake had become a very competent senior patrol leader. I did my best to ask questions rather than tell him things, and he had learned to anticipate these questions and had answers ready most of the time. I made it a habit of speaking with Jake on Wednesdays checking up on his planning and making sure the patrol leaders were contacting their Scouts.

With some coaching our patrol leaders were well on their way to becoming competent instructors and leaders; and our adults had stepped back in response to their growing abilities. My assistant Scoutmasters had kept their word, followed my lead, and were beginning to settle into their redefined roles. Adult voices in general were quieter, and seldom heard in comparison to where we had been when I started.

After our initial disagreements, our committee meetings were less of an ordeal for me, personally. Mark, our chair, had been pivotal in helping everyone work with the changes we had made.

The patrol leaders' council huddled a few minutes before and after every Monday troop meeting. The Monday night following our monthly outing was dedicated to a more formal patrol leaders' council meeting, a board of review, and Scoutmaster Conferences.

We had mostly moved from focusing on completing requirements to activities where requirements were completed almost unconsciously.

"Let me spend a few minutes with the patrol leaders' council," I replied when Eric met me at the door of our meeting room, "and then we'll sit down for your Scoutmaster's conference."

Jake had his patrol leaders gathered around a table in a corner of the meeting room.

"Any questions for me before you get going?" I asked.

"Not really," Jake replied, "the cabin trip for January is all set, right?"

"Yes, Mr. Murray made the reservations," I replied. "Like we discussed, by the time you are done this evening you'll want to have a plan for that weekend settled, and start working on what happens for the next few months."

"We are electing a new Senior Patrol Leader in February?" Jake asked.

"That's the plan," I said, "still work for you guys?"

The Scouts nodded their heads.

"I have a Scoutmaster's conference," I said, "I'll be back when you are finished, just let me know."

"We need about a half hour to go through what I have here," Jake said looking over the agenda he had prepared, "and then we need to begin getting ready for next week."

As I crossed the room, Linda, our advancement chair met me.

"One for Second Class rank?" She asked.

"I think that's what Eric is ready for," I replied, "I am on my way to do his Scoutmaster conference right now."

"Okay, we'll be ready when he is," Linda said.

Eric and I sat down, and spoke about what he'd been doing the past few months.

"You are in sixth grade this year?" I asked.

Eric nodded.

"So what's your favorite subject?" I asked.

"English, I guess." Eric replied.

"Why is that?" I asked.

Eric went on to tell me about the book he was reading, and we chatted for a while longer.

"How's things in the Fox patrol?" I continued.

"Pretty good; we have fun I guess," Eric answered.

"Would you like to be a patrol leader sometime?" I asked.

"Yeah, how do you get to do that?" he wanted to know.

"How did Bob get to be your patrol leader?" I asked.

"Oh yeah, we voted him in." Eric said, "When are we going to do that again?"

"That's up to your patrol," I told him, "you can talk about it at your next patrol meeting."

"We like Bob," Eric said, "but it would be fun to try being patrol leader."

"Well, that's really a patrol decision," I advised, "you guys should be able to figure things out; Jake can help if you need him."

"Okay," Eric agreed.

The conference went on for another five minutes or so.

"Before we finish up," I said looking in Eric's handbook, "There's one requirement that you don't have signed off here, can you read it for me?"

I handed Eric the handbook, and he began reading "Demonstrate Scout spirit by living the Scout Oath and Scout Law in your everyday life ..."

"If you were going to sign that requirement for yourself, would you?" I asked.

Eric looked at me, and thought for a moment.

"I guess, maybe?" he hesitated.

"Can you tell me why?" I continued.

"Well, I try to do good things," he answered, "like help people and be polite."

"That's good," I said, "can you tell me about a time when you did something like that?"

Eric struggled a little, but he related a couple of instances at school and at home, where he'd been helpful.

"So, on your honor as a Scout," I said, "you'd sign yourself off on that requirement?"

Eric looked at me and shrugged.

"It's not a trick question," I smiled, "you can tell me all kinds of stories about what you've done. In the end, though, you are the only one who really knows if you have lived up to the oath and law."

"I think I have, at least I try," he concluded.

"I'd agree; I think you're a good Scout," I said taking the handbook back and signing the requirement, "Mrs. Daugherty has the board of review ready for you, do you have any questions for me?"

"No, I don't think so," Eric answered.

"Well, if you have any questions or concerns you can always talk to me." I handed him his handbook and held out my hand, "Good job, Eric!"

"Thanks," he replied shaking my hand.

George, Dave, and Wayne were looking over a Scout handbook at another table, "How's it going?" I asked.

"Were working on a couple of things for Jake," Wayne replied. "They are figuring out the last few details of the cabin trip, right?"

"Yes, when I checked in with them they were just getting started," I said; "you'll be available to help them prepare?"

"We'll do our best," George said. "I hope they'll be a little farther ahead than last month."

"That's the plan," I replied, "They had a rugged meeting last week, didn't they?"

"It wasn't too bad," Wayne said; "with any luck they'll learn to avoid that again."

"There's no teacher like experience," I agreed, "it was uncomfortable to watch things kind of fall apart last week. I took the opportunity to talk to Jake; he knows how to fix things."

"Hopefully it didn't spoil things for the Scouts they are leading." George said, "That always worries me."

"The way I look at it," I replied, "if they have a stumble now and again it shows they have some real responsibility. If we aren't jumping in to fix things they get the idea it's actually up to them."

"I am getting better at keeping myself in check," George said, "it's like being in the passenger seat while the Scouts are driving."

"When I was teaching my boy to drive I had a sore foot from hitting that phantom brake," I laughed, "I know exactly what you mean."

"Mr. G.?" Jake said as he came over to our table, "We're ready for you!"

"I'll be right there," I answered, standing up.

"Hey Jake, what do you need from us?" George asked.

"In a couple of minutes could you work with Bob? He's going to do lashings." Turning to Wayne he said, "Mr. Murray, you said you could show somebody how to make rope?"

"Happy to help out," Wayne replied, "It's been a couple of years since I last did that, but we'll get it together."

"Thanks," Jake said, "I think Zach is the one who volunteered to work on that with you."

Jake and I returned to the patrol leaders' council.

After Jake went through a quick review of their plans, he turned to me, "Sound good Mr. G.?"

"So you'll be doing some pioneering during the cabin trip?" I asked.

"Yeah, we want to build a catapult," Bob explained, "It's a complicated project, but it looks like fun."

"Sounds good to me," I said, and turned to Jake, "Can we talk about last week for a minute?"

Jake nodded.

"So what happened?" I asked. "Things kind of fell apart there a little didn't they?"

Jake looked at his shoes. "Yeah, kind of."

"Happens to the best of us," I said, "don't be discouraged; you guys are doing a great job. Tell me what happened."

"We weren't ready," Hunter offered, "and we kind of made things up at the last minute."

"How did that feel?" I asked.

"Not good," Zach replied.

"Once again," I said, "let me observe how proud I am of the job all of you are doing. I am not angry or upset, not even disappointed. What's important is understanding what happened, and how it can be fixed."

"I think it was mostly because we didn't talk very much the week before," Jake admitted. "And when everybody got there we weren't ready for the meeting, and then Bob didn't show up."

"So what happened, Bob?" I asked.

"I had a lot of homework, and a test on Tuesday," Bob answered.

"So, I guess that meant somebody else had to take over for you," I said; "how much notice did they have?"

"Not much, I guess." Bob mumbled.

"Yeah, like none," Jake said, "we had to call you."

"Sorry, but I had a lot on my mind." Bob said.

"Jake you also said that you weren't really ready too, right?" I asked.

"Yeah," Jake agreed, "it wasn't all Bob's fault."

"So what's the solution?" I asked, "What will you do to avoid that sort of thing in the future?"

"We just need to talk to each other during the week," he concluded, "and follow through on our plans."

"Yeah, guys," I said, "it's really that simple. I know how frustrating this all can be, but remember, you are a great team, and you have done really, really well; don't let problems get you down. Keep communicating, encourage and support each other, and things will be fine."

"Okay," Jake said.

"That's enough from me; I said smiling; "I know you have some preparing to do, so if Jake is done, I am done."

"Everybody know what they do next?" Jake said as they all got up from the table.

As the patrol leaders headed off, Linda, our advancement chair approached. "Do you have a minute, Chuck?" she asked.

"Sure, how did things go?" I asked.

"You have a new second class Scout," she replied. "I'll have his patch next week."

"That's great!" I said. "Anything I need to know from the board?"

"Eric is doing well," Linda replied, "he's a little unsure of some of the plans for next month, he wasn't able to tell us when the next camping trip is or what they will be doing."

"Aha!" I said, "Did you fill him in?"

"Yes," She replied, "we had the information you gave us about the cabin weekend."

"Everything else seemed okay, though?" I asked.

"Yes, he's enjoying Scouts," Linda continued; "he said his favorite thing was the backpacking trip."

"That was a fun trip," I said, "one of my favorites so far. How about the things he did for requirements?"

"He thought his strongest skill was map and compass," Lind replied, "and told us a lot about that. He chose cooking as the skill he needed the most help with."

"That's interesting," I mused. "Bob, his patrol leader, has become a pretty good camp cook. I'll let Bob know that Eric needs a little help with that. Anything else?"

"No, not really; we had fun talking to him," Linda said.

"Thanks, Linda," I concluded; "I really appreciate your help!"

"I'll be sure to get that patch for next week!" Linda said.

I looked around the room abuzz with activity and realized I didn't have much else to do!

We'd had our difficulties, and there were certainly more to come. As challenging as things had been over the past few months I felt like we were finally hitting our stride.

Before long, I stood at the door, waiting for the Scouts to file out so I could lock up.

They exited laughing, talking, and roughhousing.

Eric was one of the last to leave. He ran toward a waiting car, stopped short, turned around and ran back to where I stood.

He stretched out his hand, "Thanks Mr. G.!" he said, a little out of breath.

"Thanks Eric!" I said, shaking his hand. "And congratulations!"

"Okay," he said, "thanks!"

He turned and ran towards the car, shouting "Goodnight Mr. G.!" over his shoulder.

I waved as he got in the car and headed for home.

I stood there a little stunned, wiped my eye, took a deep breath, locked the door, and turned for home myself.

So far so good!

References

Baden-Powell, Robert. **Aids to Scoutmastership**. New York and London: G. P. Putnam's Sons, 1920.

Reynolds, E. E., editor. **B.P .'s Outlook Selections from Lord Baden Powell's contributions to The Scouter**. London: C. Arthur Pearson, 1941.

41088896R00089

Made in the USA
Lexington, KY
28 April 2015